RISE OF THE CULTS

VISION HOUSE PUBLISHERS
Santa Ana, California 92705

THE RISE OF THE CULTS
Copyright © 1955, 1977 by
Walter Martin

First Printing — December, 1955
Second Printing (Revised and Enlarged) — 1957

Third Printing — 1961
Fourth Printing — 1963
Fifth Printing — 1966
Sixth Printing (Revised and Enlarged) — 1977

New International Version New Testament, copyright © 1973 by the New York Bible Society International. Used by permission.

The Revised Standard Version of the Bible copyrighted, 1946, 1952 © 1971, 1973. Used by permission.

Library of Congress Catalog Card Number 77-86536

ISBN 0-88449-070-X

Printed in the United States of America

CONTENTS

ACKNOWLEDGMENTS

In the years of development that this small volume has undergone, many people contributed to produce the present form. First thanks should go to Shelton College, First Baptist Bible School, and the periodicals *Eternity, Our Hope*, and *The Examiner*, by means of which the substance of this material was first delivered to the public as lectures and articles. I wish to express my thanks to Dr. Frank E. Gaebelein, former Headmaster of the Stony Brook School, for his patient and constructive criticisms of this work, to the late Dr. Donald Grey Barnhouse for his help through the pages of *Eternity* Magazine, and to Mr. Russell Hitt, former editor of *Eternity*, for his many fine suggestions, corrections, and useful literary assists. My thanks also to Dr. E. Schuyler English for his support and to Rev. Gilbert Peterson for his editorial assistance. Finally, my thanks to Mrs. Shiela Kenney for her fine transcription and manuscript preparation skills, and to my secretary, Mrs. Gretchen Passantino, for her efforts in helping me to update, revise, and edit this present edition.

PREFACE

Since 1955, when this work first appeared, much theological water has gone under the bridge of history. The cults and the occult were even then surging toward their great growth and tidal wave of propaganda that today, 22 years later, crests high on the ramparts of the Christian church. Fortunately, by the grace of God, I was privileged to foresee that this deluge was coming, and I sought to warn the church that we must be prepared to meet and resist the rise of the cults and the occult, while never forgetting the task of evangelizing those caught within their webs of deception. History and experience tell us that the twofold ministry of the church—evangelism and the defense of the gospel—can be effectively realized and implemented. Unfortunately and to my sorrow, that warning went largely unheeded, and I was described as an "alarmist." The public was told that the cults were not outpacing the church. However, this was not the case, as any student of the last decade well knows. Today a virulent cultic and occultic revival is sweeping our country, dating from approximately 1965; much of the world has now begun to feel its powerful impact. But there is a real ray of hope in this dark picture: the Lord has begun to arouse His people.

Thinking Christians now realize that the danger to them, their children, and their grandchildren is real, not imagined. They have also become aware that cultists and occultists can be successfully answered and evangelized, thus turning enemies of the gospel into stalwart Christians. I have never regretted being right about anything quite so much in my entire ministry. I wish it had been otherwise; I wish that just preaching the gospel without defending the faith effectively and evangelizing the cults directly would have contained the rise of the cults. But the contrary facts are before us on every side. The cults simply will not go away, and neither can they any longer be ignored or drowned in a sea of evasive rhetoric, statistics, or argument. The rise of the cults is upon us with a vengeance at home and on every major world mission field.

The response of the church must be immediate and positive if this rise is to be checked and perhaps contained, though this now will take an act of sovereign grace because of the enormous multiplication and proliferation of cultic structures. The time for talk is over; the time for *action* in the name of the gospel has arrived. In a word, the challenge is here, the time is *now*.

This revised edition is sent forth with the earnest hope and prayer that those who read it and may belong to any of the cultic systems herein described may see, by contrast with Holy Scripture, their personal need of Jesus Christ— the Christ of divine revelation, not cultic imagination—as Savior and Lord. We also pray that interested students of contemporary cultism may catch a glimpse of a great mission field to be evangelized for the Lord. My wish is that we may be encouraged to a deeper study of the Word of God and be stimulated to a more effective proclamation of His gospel and defense of His faith, "For with God nothing shall be impossible."

Walter Martin, San Juan Capistrano
California, 1977

A COMMENDATION

from

Dr. Wilbur M. Smith

Apart from sheer unbelief and the deep paganism of our modern civilization, the greatest hindrance to an acceptance of the saving gospel of Jesus Christ is the teaching of these false cults, which, on the periphery of Christianity, deceivingly and inaccurately use many of the sacred terms of the true Christian faith. These cults are spreading with phenomenal speed, and by them millions are being led astray. The world as such, of course, can never be expected to expose the evil roots and false teachings of these religions—this can be expected only from those who know the Word of God and the truth as it is in Christ. The danger is that too many in the church, unacquainted with and really uninterested in the history and actual teachings of these groups, are lulled into a state of indifference toward them, or, even worse, into believing that these false religions are also a true way to God, whereas they lead to nothing else but eternal death.

No man in America today has carried on such extended, careful research in this important area of contemporary religious life as has Dr. Walter Martin. After collaborating with Norman Klann on a number of articles and two excellent volumes, *Jehovah of the Watchtower* and *The Christian Science Myth*, Dr. Martin has brought together the results of his years of study in this comprehensive work, *The Rise of the Cults*. This is the most significant work on cults to appear in this country in the last twenty years, and it is certainly the only one that is up-to-date now.

One

CULTISM TODAY

It has been wisely observed that the field of apologetics has the depth of the oceans and the breadth of the celestial galaxies. This very fact in itself must serve to indicate that this book is not meant to encompass so vast a realm of knowledge.

The scope of this book is the field of contemporary American cults, and most particularly seven of the major cults which today challenge evangelical Christianity both at home and on the various mission fields of the world. These seven cults include Jehovah's Witnesses, Mormonism, Christian Science, the Unity School of Christianity, Spiritism, Baha'ism, and Herbert Armstrong's World-Wide Church of God. I have also included in this survey the Dawn Bible Students (the original followers of Charles Taze Russell) grouped together with Jehovah's Witnesses.

Perhaps it is best to begin our study of these cults by defining precisely what we mean when we attach the label of "cult" to a particular organization, so that as we progress into the field we shall not be hampered by the problem of fluctuating terminology.

Today on the mission fields of the world, and indeed on every street corner of the major cities of the six continents, cultism is on the march.

By cultism we mean the adherence to major doctrines which are pointedly contradictory to orthodox Christianity, yet which claim the distinction of either tracing their origin to orthodox sources or of being in essential harmony with those sources. Cultism, in short, is *any major deviation from orthodox Christianity relative to the cardinal doctrines of the Christian faith.* A cult, then, is a group of people polarized around someone's interpretation of the Bible and is characterized by major deviations from orthodox Christianity relative to the cardinal doctrines of the Christian faith, particularly the fact that God became man in Jesus Christ. Thus we see the Mormons polarized around Joseph Smith and Brigham Young, Christian Scientists around Mary Baker Eddy, and the other groups around their respective leaders.

The most prominent among the cults are Jehovah's Witnesses, Mormonism, Christian Science, Unity, and Herbert Armstrong's World-Wide Church of God. All of these deny both the Biblical doctrines of the Trinity and the deity of Jesus Christ. Numerically, these five cults have a following *exceeding 8.5 million persons,*[1] as well as missionary programs which circle the globe in ever-increasing numbers. Jehovah's Witnesses alone boast well over 226,-500 "missionaries" in the New York metropolitan area, and at one of their International Conventions held in New York City's Yankee Stadium, the zealous Witnesses filled both the Stadium (85,000) and the neighboring Polo Grounds (50,000) to overflowing. Beyond this astonishing and alarming fact, Jehovah's Witnesses have 96 branches circulating their literature in 160 languages to 270 lands, literally denying from pole to pole the Trinity and the deity of Jesus Christ, His physical resurrection and visible return to judge the world.

Christian Science, on the other hand, has concentrated on reaching the larger centers of world population; few indeed are those cities where Christian Science churches and reading rooms are not conspiciously in evidence. Through the excellent propaganda efforts of their three chief publications, the *Christian Science Monitor, Sentinel,* and *Journal,* the Christian Science religion has managed to gain for

---

[1]The breakdown of numbers is as follows: Jehovah's Witnesses, 2,000,000; Christian Science, 400,000-600,000; Mormonism, 3,500,000; Herber W. Armstrong, 75,000; Unity, 2,500,000.

itself a position and reputation that Mrs. Eddy was completely incapable of endowing it with, and has won acceptance among many uninformed sources as a nominally Christian religion. However, nothing could be further from the actual truth of the matter, for in reality Christian Science denies virtually every cardinal doctrine of the Christian faith, not only those previously mentioned, but many others far too numerous to record in this overview chapter. Christian Science practitioners (Mrs. Eddy's inadequate substitution for qualified medical doctors) as of January 1974 numbered over five thousand, many of whom sometimes command prestige equal to that of qualified medical men. The Armed Forces have also accepted Christian Science chaplains! Whereas Jehovah's Witnesses are for the most part outwardly respectful of Biblical authority, the disciples of Mrs. Eddy deny the absolute authority of the Scriptures outright and are not in the least disturbed by the implication of their attitude.[2]

In contrast to both Jehovah's Witnesses and Christian Science, The Church of Jesus Christ of Latter-day Saints, or the Mormons, has incorporated the prime traits of the others, emphasizing both metropolitan and rural propaganda work in a renewed attempt to rout evangelical Christianity from world mission fields regardless of location. From their focal point of distribution in Salt Lake City, the eager disciples of Joseph Smith and Brigham Young have increasingly widened their sphere of missionary influence. The new fifteen-million-dollar Mormon Temple erected in Washington, D. C., and the various Mormon wards springing up all over the United States bear pointed testimony to the rapid rise of the Latter-day Saints. Mormonism (as with all the previously mentioned cults) capitalizes upon the reverence most people have for the Bible, a reverence not always based upon what lies within the seldom-opened covers. Many well-meaning persons

---

[2]See *Miscellaneous Writings*, Mary Baker Eddy, ed., 1897, pp. 169, 170, etc.

have that peculiar kind of faith which parallels that of the man who buried a box of fruit for the winter in the belief that the frost would preserve it. He loudly insisted that his was the best fruit in the country, but upon digging it up in the spring he found it rotten and spoiled by the rigorous climatic changes of the season. Likewise many people bury their faith, firmly insisting that it is sound, yet never bothering to dig it up or examine it to see if it has been affected by the conditions and demands of life. It is upon this type of person that cultism feeds, devouring in ever-increasing numbers those who are not sure what they believe or why they believe it.

Moving on to the Unity School of Christianity, we are struck with the similarity of its approach and theology to that of Christian Science. Charles and Myrtle Fillmore, the founders of Unity, sought physical health and monetary remuneration, both of which they obtained by convincing over two million persons that "sickness" and "death" are illusions, and that the bodily resurrection and the deity of our Lord are unnecessary doctrines.[3] Negating, as it does, the authority of the Bible, and spiritualizing whatever texts are found to be embarrassing, Unity, like Christian Science, has built a multimillion-dollar business upon the false premises that God is impersonal, that sin and sickness are largely illusory, and that Unity is the true Christian religion.

When surveying these problems, therefore, it is vitally essential that we understand one of the basic causes of cultism: *the unfortunate failure of the church to institute and emphasize a definite, systematic plan of cult evangelism and apologetic and doctrinal theology.* The average Christian is, sad to say, terribly unprepared to defend his faith thoroughly. In a word, he knows *what* he believes, but too often he does not know *why.* This fact is the chink in the armor of othodoxy into which the cults have driven a subtle wedge, and through which innumerable false doctrines

---

[3]See Chapter 6 of this book.

have penetrated with alarming rapidity and telling effect.

It is also helpful to remember, when dealing with cults, that whatever variety one may encounter, *cults are always built, not upon what the Bible teaches, but upon what the founders of the respective cults said the Bible teaches.* So in the final analysis it is necessary to refute the claims of the cult founders in order to effectively undermine faith in the related cult.

Cultism thrives principally upon two factors: *ignorance* and *uncertainty.* Where these most abound, there cultism will also be found in force. The cults consistently appeal to "reason" and "rationality," which many times they use as their sole guide in evaluating the character of God and His revelation. Hell is "unreasonable," eternal punishment is "irrational," consciousness after death is a "pagan theory," and therefore these doctrines could not be true, argue the cults, apparently oblivious to the fact that they are circumscribing the infinite God to the scope of their finite reasoning processes and imputing to Him their manifestly feeble powers of logical thought.

Most cult adherents assume God to be what they believe He should be, but Scripture tells us repeatedly that He is not to be measured by our limited abilities, but by what He has declared in His Word (Isaiah 55:8; cp. Romans 11:33-36). The rise of the cults is therefore directly proportional to the fluctuating emphasis which the Christian church has placed on the teaching of Biblical doctrine to Christian laymen. To be sure, a few pastors, teachers, and evangelists defend adequately their beliefs, but most of them and most of the average Christian laymen are hard put to confront and refute a well-trained cultist of almost any variety. *The shock troops of cultism are surprise and confusion.* Cultists surprise the Christian by apparent mastery of his own textbook, the Bible, and confuse him with glib quotations, usually completely out of context, which appear to challenge the most cherished of orthodox tenets. " 'My Father is greater than I' (John 14:28) proves that Jesus was not God," says the self-assured Jehovah's Witness; "God is

Love—how can he punish us?" echoes the Christian Scientist. The cultists maintain that all these statements are strongly supported by various Scripture verses—quoted mostly out of context and thoroughly mystifying to many concerned but unprepared Christians.

In the case of the more subtle cult propagandists, such as specially trained representatives of the Watch Tower Bible and Tract Society, *a veneer of scholarship plays a part of major importance.* The well-trained Jehovah's Witness sprinkles his discourses with frequent references to the original languages of the Bible (Hebrew, Aramaic, and Greek), when it is a matter of known fact that less than one-half of one percent of the best-trained Jehovah's Witnesses knows anything, scholastically speaking, of these languages beyond the alphabet stage.

Regarding the Watch Tower Society's translations of the Bible,[4] it should be understood that their "translation committee" (consisting of no known scholars) has ventured almost no interest in either correcting or defending the numerous outright perversions and errors so evident in their translations. This is the case despite invitations by qualified Hebrew and Greek scholars for them to do so. However, *very few Christians know enough to dig beneath these deceptive veneers of pseudoscholarship,* and hence the smooth-talking representatives of "Pastor" Russell's "theocracy" continue to succeed in their task of bluffing Christians into silence with the arrogant pretension that the Watch Tower Bible and Tract Society's translations are always based upon competent scholarship.[5]

Keeping pace with the rapid rise of cult propaganda in written form has been the cultists' use of the media of television and radio, as particularly displayed in the activities of Unity, Christian Science, and Jehovah's Witnesses. The

---

[4]*The New World Translation of the Scriptures* and *The Kingdom Interlinear Translation of the Christian Greek Scriptures.*

[5]See *The Scholastic Dishonesty of the Watchtower* and *The Sandcastle of Jehovah' Witnesses,* by Michael Van Buskirk, CARIS, Box 1783, Santa Ana, California 92702.

Russellite program "Frank and Ernest" (theologically the forerunner of the present Watch Tower group) is broadcast coast-to-coast every week. Unfortunately, in the recent past, if a cult "sounded" orthodox, most Christians never took the trouble to investigate it; rather, they tended to ignore it, and in so doing encouraged its expansion, a fact which today they most openly deplore.

Just how can this problem be solved effectively? I discuss this in Chapter 9, but we should never forget that the growth of cults is a true sign of the end of the ages, when "deceivers shall grow worse and worse, deceived and being deceived . . . ever learning and never able to come to a knowledge of the truth." In the great Olivet discourse of Matthew 24, concerning the second coming of Christ and the end of the ages, this sign was mentioned more than any of the others. Christ three times stressed that in the end times false Christs and false prophets would arise and deceive many (Matthew 24:5, 11, 24). We are being called today to believe in the urgency of the second coming of Christ, and we are constantly reminded of Israel and other current events in the light of Biblical prophecy. We must direct our attention, then, to the fact that Jesus Christ gave the ultimate sign. That ultimate sign is the proliferation of cult teaching and cult doctrine. Let us therefore as ambassadors of Christ "put on the whole armour of God . . . , for we wrestle not against flesh and blood, but against the rulers of the darkness of this world, against spiritual wickedness in heavenly places" (Ephesians 6:11, 12). God grant that now in this hour of decision we may be "strong in the Lord, and in the power of His might."

Two

JEHOVAH'S WITNESSES

On February 16, 1852, in the state of Pennsylvania, just outside Pittsburgh, a son was born to Joseph L. Russell and his wife, Anna Eliza, and was subsequently christened Charles Taze Russell. Young Russell spent most of his boyhood in the area known as Allegheny, a suburb of Pittsburgh, where at the age of 25 he had become a successful businessman. Charles Russell was a Congregationalist by denomination and, from what is known of his early history, a zealous but poorly educated student of the Bible. It was as a direct result of his interest in Biblical things that Russell in 1870 organized a Bible study group, which in 1876 elected him "pastor." By this time "Pastor" Russell had totally rejected many of the cardinal doctrines of historic Christianity, such as the Trinity, the deity of Christ, Christ's physical resurrection and return, and the doctrine of eternal retribution for sin.

In 1879 "Pastor" Russell[1] invested some of his hard-earned savings in a small magazine, *Zion's Watch Tower*, which in later years became *The Watchtower Announcing Jehovah's Kingdom* (now the official organ of Jehovah's Witnesses). Russell followed this move by forming Zion's Watch Tower Tract Society in 1884 (later The Watch Tower Bible and Tract Society), which in 1886 published the first in a series of seven books (Russell wrote six of them) entitled *The Millennial Dawn*. This title was later changed to *Studies in the Scriptures*, owing to the concentrated criticisms of the Christian clergy against the Millennial Dawn movement.

---

[1] He was never officially ordained in the common acceptance of the term.

The first edition of *Zion's Watch Tower* was 6,000 copies per month; today *The Watchtower*, its great grandchild, distributes 18 million copies per month in 78 languages worldwide! Another of *The Watchtower's* publications is *Awake* magazine, with a circulation of over 14.3 million in 67 languages! The actual membership of Jehovah's Witnesses today exceeds 2 million members, and the organization is represented by branches in more than 207 lands.

In 1908 "Pastor" Russell moved his headquarters to Brooklyn, New York, where a huge printing operation was undertaken. After 69 years of activity this press has produced billions of pieces of literature. Today, owing largely to Russell's foresight, The Watch Tower Bible and Tract Society owns, among other things, whole blocks of valuable property in downtown Brooklyn, a large printing plant, a "Kingdom farm," and a missionary training school—Gilead—located in South Lansing, New York.

"Pastor" Russell continued his varied activities until his death in 1916 aboard a transcontinental train in Texas. His death brought to a close a most remarkable life, and one that will long be remembered in the annals of American cultism.

Charles Taze Russell might have been one of the great evangelists of the Christian church had he subjugated his reasoning powers to the Holy Spirit, but instead he chose to crusade against the historical church and its doctrine, and so died an unrewarding death.

Russell's career was also highly colored with moral and legal scandal, notably so in 1903, when Mrs. Russell (whom he married in 1880 and who had left him after seventeen years of marriage in 1897) sued the "Pastor" for divorce and was awarded a separation in 1906, following sensational testimony as to the "Pastor's" questionable habits with another woman, Rose Ball. In 1909 Russell was forced to pay his wife $6,036 in back alimony after it was shown that he deliberately transferred his property holdings to avoid payment.

Further than this, "Pastor" Russell once sued the Reverend J. J. Ross of Hamilton, Ontario, for libel over a pamphlet the latter had written, only to lose the case and prove himself a perjurer on the witness stand.[2] Much, much more could be cited to show that Charles Taze Russell was not the caliber of man to trust in things of the Spirit, but despite this his writings had a circulation of 25 million copies, and *The Watchtower* of today still owns him as its founder and spreads many of his teachings. Jehovah's Witnesses of today, however, obtained their name from J. F. Rutherford, better known as the "Judge," in 1931. As Russell's trusted lawyer, Rutherford took over the movement in 1916 and ran it without question until his death from cancer in 1942. Frederick W. Franz today pilots *The Watchtower*, and he continues in the same path as the "Pastor" and the Judge, both of whom have for the most part faded into *The Watchtower's* lengthening shadow.

THE DAWN BIBLE STUDENTS

As is frequently the case with cults of all varieties, they are often rent apart by schism, and Jehovah's Witnesses are no exception.

Shortly after the death of "Pastor Russell" and continuing on till 1929, there was a gradual but definite schism in the theocratic fold, with one group holding fast to Russell's doctrines and the other adhering to the "expanded teachings" of Judge Rutherford. The final split came in the late twenties, when Rutherford abandoned Russell's pyramid system of prophecy and gave an ultimatum to the Russellites. The ultimatum in due time was thrown back into his honor's teeth in the form of a new organization founded upon Russell's teachings exclusively, and titled *The Dawn Bible Students*.

---

[2] For a thorough discussion of the entire Jehovah's Witnesses movement, see Walter Martin, *Jehovah of the Watchtower* (8th. edition, revised and enlarged. Chicago: Moody Press, 1975).

From meager beginnings in the depression era, the Dawn movement today boasts a coast-to-coast radio program, "Frank and Ernest," a good-sized printing establishment in East Rutherford, New Jersey, the cult's headquarters, and a magazine, *The Dawn*. Compared to Jehovah's Witnesses' huge printing accomplishments, this is small indeed, but the Dawn movement is growing, and cannot be ignored by thoughtful persons.

The Dawnites agree 95 percent with the Jehovah's Witnesses on all major doctrines, rejecting only Rutherford's innovations and holding to a "second chance" for unregenerate men should they reject Christ now (in the tradition of "Pastor" Russell).

The Watchtower, on the other hand, has condemned the Dawnites, calling them the "evil servant" class, and has claimed for the Witnesses independence from Russell's theology—which brings us to our next point.

One of the most distressing traits manifested in the literature and teachings of Jehovah's Witnesses is their seeming disregard for historical facts and dependable literary consistency, while at the same time vilifying all religious opponents as "enemies of God"[3] and perpetrators of what they term "a racket."[4]

For some time now I have been considerably disturbed by Jehovah's Witnesses' constant denial of any theological connection whatsoever with "Pastor" Charles T. Russell, their admitted founder and the first president of the Watch Tower Bible and Tract Society. Since Russell was long ago proved to be a perjurer under oath, a sworn enemy of historical Christianity, and a scholastic fraud of long standing, it is obvious why the Witnesses seek to avoid his influence and memory whenever possible. Be that as it may, however, some light should be thrown on the repeated self-contradictions which are committed by the Witnesses in their zeal to justify their position and the ever-wavering

---

[3] J. F. Rutherford, *Deliverance*, p. 91. Also *Religion*, pp. 263, 268.
[4] *Religion*, pp. 88, 104, 133, 137, 140, 141, etc.

doctrines to which they hold. It is our contention that they are following the basic teachings of Charles T. Russell in relation to many Biblical doctrines which he denied, and from their own publication we shall document this accusation, painful as it may be to *The Watchtower*.

In their eagerness to repudiate the charge of "Russellism," the Witnesses dogmatically say: ". . . but who is preaching the teaching of Pastor Russell? *Certainly not* Jehovah's Witnesses! They cannot be accused of following him, for they *neither quote him as an authority nor publish nor distribute his writings.*"[5] This is the statement of the Witnesses' magazine. Now let us compare this with history, and the truth will be plainly revealed.

Historically, Jehovah's Witnesses have quoted "Pastor" Russell innumerable times since his death in 1916. The following is a token sample of what we can produce as concrete evidence. In 1923, seven years after the "Pastor's" demise, Judge J. F. Rutherford, then heir-apparent to the Russellite throne, wrote a booklet some fifty-odd pages in length entitled *World Distress—Why and the Remedy*. In this informative treatise, the new president of The Watch Tower Bible and Tract Society and the International Bible Students quoted "Pastor" Russell no less than sixteen separate times; referred to his books *Studies in the Scriptures* over twelve times; and devoted six pages at the end of the booklet to advertising these same volumes. Further than this, in a 57-page pamphlet published in 1925 and entitled *Comfort for the People*, the same Rutherford in true Russellite character defines clergymen as "dumb dogs (D. D.)," proceeds to quote "Pastor" Russell's prophetical chronology (A.D. 1914)[6] and then sums up his tirade against Christendom universal by recommending Russell's writings in four pages of advertisements at the rear of the book.

---

[5] *Awake*, May 8, 1951, p. 26.

[6] Jehovah's Witnesses still hold to this today and teach it as a dogma.

The dark specter of historical facts thus begins to creep across the previously happy picture of a "Russell-free"[7] movement. But let us further consult history. In the year 1927, The Watch Tower Bible and Tract Society published Judge Rutherford's "great" literary effort entitled *Creation*, which was circulated into the millions of copies, and in which this statement appeared concerning "Pastor" Russell:

> The second presence of Christ dates from about 1874.
>
> From that time forward many of the truths long obscured by the enemy began to be restored to the honest Christian.
>
> As William Tyndale was used to bring the Bible to the attention of the people, so the Lord used Charles T. Russell to bring to the attention of the people an understanding of the Bible, particularly of those truths that had been taken away by the machinations of the Devil and his agencies. Because it was the Lord's due time to restore these truths, He used Charles T. Russell to write and publish books known as *Studies in the Scriptures*, by which the great fundamental truths of the divine plan are clarified. Satan has done his best to destroy these books because they *explain* the Scriptures. Even as Tyndale's Version of the Bible was destroyed by the clergy, so the clergy in various parts of the earth have gathered together thousands of volumes of *Studies in Scriptures* and burned them publicly. But such wickedness has only served to advertise the truth of the divine plan.

Please consider, if you will, this statement by the then-president of the Jehovah's Witnesses organization. Rutherford plainly quotes Russell and his writings as authoritative material, yet *The Watchtower* today claims that Jehovah's

---

[7] Jehovah's Witnesses have been forced to openly acknowledge Russell, owing to the effect of my book *Jehovah of the Watchtower*, which gave the true history of Russell's infamous doings, thus necessitating an answer from the Witnesses, even if it was an unreliable one in many respects and highly colored in Watchtower fashion. The historical series was run in *The Watchtower* for some months and was entitled "A Modern History of Jehovah's Witnesses." A new history, recently published, is entitled *Jehovah's Witnesses in the Divine Purpose*.

Witnesses are free from the taint of "Russellism." Once again history weighs the dependability of Jehovah's Witnesses and finds it wanting.

Concluding this brief historical synopsis of the Watch Tower Society's past, we quote the grand finale of J. F. Rutherford's funeral oration over the prostrate remains of "dear Brother Russell," who, according to the floral sign by his casket, remained "faithful unto death." As to just what he was faithful to, Rutherford never did comment. Said the Judge: "Our brother sleeps not in death, but was instantly changed from the human to the divine nature, and is now forever with the Lord." This episode in Jehovah's Witnesses' history is cited for its uniqueness, to show the adoration in which Russell was once held by the theological ancestors of those who deny his influence today.

Leaving the past history of the Witnesses, I shall now answer those who say: "The Society may have quoted him in the past, but that was before Judge Rutherford's death. We do not do it now, and after all, didn't we say 'neither quote . . . publish . . . nor distribute his writings'? This is in the *present* tense, not the past." This would, I agree, be a splendid refutation of our claims if it were true, but is it? Not only did Jehovah's Witnesses quote the "Pastor" as an authority in the past, before Rutherford's death in 1942, but they have kept right on doing so after his death and on to the present.

In the July 15, 1950, edition of *The Watchtower* (p. 216), the Witnesses quoted "Pastor" Russell as an authority regarding his chronology on the 2,520-year-reign of the Gentiles, which reign allegedly ended, according to his calculations (and Jehovah's Witnesses'), in A.D. 1914.[8] To make the contradiction even more hopeless, they listed as their source *The Watch-Tower* of 1880, of which "Pastor" Russell was editor-in-chief! Now if they "do not consider his

---

[8] See *Apostles of Denial*, by Edmund Gruss (Nutley, N. J.: Presbyterian and Reformed Publishing Co., 1970) for a thorough refutation of Jehovah's Witnesses' prophetic falsehoods.

writings authoritative and do not circulate them," why publish his chronology, quote his publication, and admit his teachings on this vital point in their theology? The answer is simple. They have contradicted themselves whether or not they admit it, thus proving that they have misrepresented the truth and have denied all along what they know to be absolute facts.

To shatter any misconception as to their literary honesty, we refer the interested reader to a six-page pamphlet published by *The Watchtower* and entitled *Jehovah's Witnesses, Communists or Christians?* (1953). Throughout the major content of this propaganda, Jehovah's Witnesses defend the thesis that they are not Communists (which they are not), but, in their zeal to prove "their skirts clean," they quote "Pastor" Russell's writings no less than five times, refer to them with pride twice (pp. 4, 5), and even mention two of his best-known works, *The Plan of the Ages* (1886) and *The Battle of Armageddon* (1897). Further than this, The Watchtower of October 1, 1953, quotes "Pastor" Russell's *Studies in the Scriptures* (Vol. IV, p. 554) and Judge Rutherford's *Vindication* (Vol. II, p. 311)—convincing evidence indeed that *The Watchtower* still follows the Russellite theology of its founder. All this despite the fact that they say, in their own words, "Jehovah's Witnesses . . . neither quote him [Russell] as an authority nor publish nor distribute his writings" (*Awake*, May 8, 1951, p. 26). As a further point to ponder, it is a fact that as recently as 1975 *The Watchtower* mentioned and quoted "Pastor" Russell as its founder and as the originator of basic Watchtower theology.[9]

I leave the final judgment to the fairness of the interested reader, who, I feel confident, cannot help but see that Charles Taze Russell still speaks through *The Watchtower* of today as he did in the past.

---

[9] See the Watchtower publications *God's Kingdom of 1,000 Years Has Approached* and the *1975 Yearbook* article, "History of the Watchtower."

THE THEOLOGY OF RUSSELLISM

The basic Christological tenet of Jehovah's Witnesses, or Russellism, is that utilized by the old Alexandrian theologian, Arius, in the third century, and which subsequently won for him the "distinction" of excommunication from the Christian church at the Council of Nicea in A.D. 325.

Like Arius, whom he emulated, Russell and the Jehovah's Witnesses rejected the doctrine of the Trinity as "a false doctrine promulgated by Satan for the purpose of defaming Jehovah's name."[10] In place of the Trinity, the Witnesses accept Jesus as "a second god" or "a god," the first and greatest creation of Jehovah God.[11]

For Jehovah's Witnesses, the Lord Jesus was the archangel Michael prior to His arrival on earth, and while He was on earth He was only a perfect man who merited immortality by obedience to Jehovah's commands.[12]

Such a view is, of course, totally unscriptural, and has been thoroughly refuted in my book *Jehovah of the Watchtower*, along with all the other antibiblical teachings of Jehovah's Witnesses.

For those who are interested in an exhaustive treatment of the subject, I recommend the lengthy chapter on Jehovah's Witnesses in my book, *Kingdom of the Cults*, which covers many of the major American cult systems.

In concluding this outline of Russellism or Jehovah's Witnesses, I have listed the following major doctrines of the movement, documented from the literature of the cult itself. These are verbatim quotations, not hearsay, and are therefore authentic and dependable.

---

[10] J. F. Rutherford, *Uncovered*, Watch Tower Bible and Tract Society, 1934.

[11] See John 1:1 in *The New World Translation of the Christian Greek Scriptures*.

[12] See *Awake*, June 22, 1955, p. 9.

The Trinity

This is what they think Christians believe concerning the Trinity: "The doctrine, in brief, is that there are three gods in one: God the Father, God the Son, and God the Holy Ghost, all three equal in power, substance and eternity" (*Let God Be True,* p. 81, 1946 edition).[13]

1. "The obvious conclusion therefore is that Satan is the originator of the 'trinity doctrine,' " (*op. cit.*, p. 82).
2. "The 'trinity doctrine' was not conceived by Jesus or the early Christians" (*op. cit.*, p. 92).

The Deity of Jesus Christ

1. " . . . The true Scriptures speak of God's Son, the Word, as 'a god.' He is a 'mighty god,' but not 'the Almighty God, who is Jehovah'—Isaiah 9:6" (*The Truth Shall Make You Free*, p. 47).
2. "In other words, he [Christ] was the first and direct creation of Jehovah God. . . . He was the start of God's creative work" (*The Kingdom Is at Hand*, pp. 46, 47, 49).

The Atonement of Christ

1. "That which is redeemed is *that which was lost,* namely, perfect human life with its rights and earthly propects" (*Let God Be True*, p. 96).

The Resurrection of Christ

1. "The firstborn one [Christ] from the dead was not raised out of the grave a human creature but he was raised a spirit" (*op. cit.*, p. 272).
2. "So the King Christ Jesus was put to death in the flesh and was resurrected an invisible spirit creature" (*op. cit.*, p. 122).

The Return of Christ

They claim it has already occurred invisibly in 1914-1918.

---

[13] Unless otherwise stated, this thirteenth edition is meant.

1. "It does not mean that he [Christ] is on the way or has promised to come, but that he has already arrived" (*op. cit.*, pp. 187, 188).
2. "Christ Jesus came, not as a human, but as a glorious spirit creature" (*op. cit.*, p. 185).

Human Government

1. "Jehovah's Witnesses do not salute the flag of any nation" (*op. cit.*, p. 234).
2. "Any national flag is a symbol or image of the sovereign power of that nation" (*op. cit.*, p. 235).

The Existence of Hell and Eternal Punishment

1. "It is so plain that in the Bible Hell is the tomb, the grave, that even an honest little child can understand it, but not the religious theologians" (*op. cit.*, pp. 72).
2. " . . . God-dishonoring religious doctrine . . . " (*op. cit.*, p. 68).
3. "The doctrine of a burning hell where the wicked are tortured eternally after death cannot be true, mainly for four reasons: (1) Because it is wholly unscriptural; (2) Because it is unreasonable; (3) Because it is contrary to God's love; and (4) Because it is repugnant to justice" (*op. cit.*, p. 80).
4. " . . . The promulgator of it is Satan Himself. . . . " (*op. cit.*, p. 79).

Satan—The Devil

1. "The ultimate end of Satan is complete annihilation" (*op. cit.*, p. 55).

The Existence of The Soul

1. " . . . Man is a combination of two things, namely, the 'dust of the ground' and 'the breath of life.' The combining of these two things (or elements) produced a living soul or creature man" (*op. cit.*, p. 59).
2. "Thus we see that the claim of religionists that man has an immortal soul, and therefore differs from the beast, is not Scriptural" (*op. cit.*, pp. 59, 60).

3. "Thus it is seen that the serpent (the Devil) is the one who originated the doctrine of the inherent immortality of the soul" (*op. cit.*, p. 66).

The Kingdom of Heaven

1. "The undefeatable purpose of Jehovah God to establish a righteous kingdom in these last days was fulfilled A.D. 1914" (*op. cit.*, p. 128).
2. "Who, and how many, are able to enter the Kingdom? Revelation limits the number to 144,000 that become a part of the Kingdom and stand on Mount Zion— Revelation 14:1, 3; 7:4-8" (*op. cit.*, p. 121).

In the light of these obvious denials of Scripture and Christianity, the interested Christian and non-Christian alike might well take warning about this counterfeit of Christ's gospel. Jehovah's Witnesses or the Watch Tower Bible and Tract Society is no more than another name for Russellism, the teachings of Charles Taze Russell, a false scholar and religious imposter who made merchandise of the Christian faith. Jehovah's Witnesses, of course, maintain that they do not follow "Pastor" Russell, but this is a deliberate falsehood, as has been shown by their doctrines and their references to him and his writings. The end product of this cult is a subtle denial of our Lord Jesus Christ—His true deity, resurrection, and return. The Witnesses have never ceased to dishonor Him regarding these points of revelation, making a mere creature of God's eternal Son who died for all men to purchase for us a home in heaven, not a Russellite paradise on earth.

Listed below are the corresponding verses from the Bible on the ten points of Jehovah's Witnesses doctrine previously quoted, which will, we believe, refute beyond reasonable doubt the Witnesses' jumbled Russellism.[14]

1. *The Trinity:* Isaiah 48:16; Genesis 1:26; 11:7; 18:2, 3; Isaiah 6:8; Matthew 28:19; John 14:16; 2 Corinthians 13:14.

---

[14] For a more detailed refutation and exposition of the entire movement, consult *Jehovah of the Watchtower*, especially Chapter III.

2. *The Deity of Christ:* John 1:1; 5:18; 8:58; 10:28; 17:15; Philippians 2:8-11; Colossians 2:9; Hebrews 1:1-4.

3. *The Atonement:* John 1:29; Revelation 13:8; Leviticus 17:11; Hebrews 9:22; 1 Peter 2:24; Colossians 1:20; 2 Corinthians 5:20.

4. *The Return of Christ* (Visible): Matthew 24:30; Revelation 1:7; 1 Thessalonians 4:16, 17; Zechariah 12:10.

5. *The Resurrection of Christ* (Bodily): John 20:27, 28; Luke 24:39-44; Mark 16:14; 1 Corinthians 15:15.

6. *Human Government:* Romans 13:1-7.

7. *The Existence of Hell and Eternal Punishment:* Matthew 5:22; 8:11, 12; 13:42, 50; 2 Peter 2:17; Jude 13.

8. *Satan—The Devil:* Matthew 25:41; Revelation 20:10; etc.

9. *The Existence of the Soul:* Genesis 1:26; 5:1; 1 Corinthians 11:7; Job 32:8; Acts 7:59; 2 Corinthians 4:12.

10. *The Kingdom of Heaven:* Luke 17:20-26; Revelation 22:1-5, 14.

Three

ARMSTRONG'S WORLD CHURCH OF GOD

The rise of the World Wide Church of God is one of the truly phenomenal stories in the growth of American cultism. Beginning in 1934 under the direction of its founder, Herbert W. Armstrong, it continues today (more than forty years later) to be the fastest-growing, most financially secure, and most vocal of all indigenous American cult systems.

Though Herbert Armstrong is now an octagenarian, he still has a major voice in the policies and teachings of the church he founded. However, the real power in what has been termed "the Armstrong empire" is his dynamic, personable, and highly persuasive successor in back of the microphone and in front of the TV cameras, Garner Ted Armstrong. I think it may be said without contradiction that Garner Ted is a master of communications and knows how to utilize the media advantageously in the spreading of his religion. Of all the cultic structures, the World Wide Church of God sponsors more radio broadcasts and television programs on more stations than any other cultic group in the world, and in fact more than its five top competitors combined![1] Herbert W. Armstrong has made it a career to become a senior statesman of diplomacy for his church, and visits the various leaders of established and emerging nations, attracting their attention by his expen-

---

[1] Exact figures were asked for from Dan Ricker of Armstrong's *World-Wide Advertising*, but he was extremely uncooperative and refused to give statistics.

sive gifts and direct-aid programs in areas where the individual country may be in need.

An example of Armstrong's diplomacy is his high standing with the Israeli government, for whom he has sponsored archeological digs, not the least of which are his much-publicized excavations around and underneath the site of the second temple in Jerusalem.

The Armstrong religion is strong in England, throughout the United Kingdom, and on the European continent, as well as in the United States. It should be noted that Radio Luxembourg and other stations beam Mr. Armstrong's material all over Europe and behind the Iron Curtain, so the work of the church is not strange to them.

One of the greatest mistakes the Christian church has made in relation to Mr. Armstrong is that it has not recognized his mastery of the world of communications and the persuasiveness of his eclectic theology.

Herbert Armstrong was influenced in his early days by the Seventh-Day Adventists' denomination and also by the writings of Charles Russell, founder of the Watchtower Bible and Tract Society, better known today as Jehovah's Witnesses. Though Armstrong vigorously denies any influence from outside sources relative to his doctrines, one need only listen to Garner Ted for a period of one or two months and the roots of his theological thought emerge quite clearly.

One of the reasons why it is so difficult to pin Mr. Armstrong's errors down is that he sounds like Billy Graham when he says "Jesus is God" one week; the next week, like Mormonism: "you can become divine"; the next week like the original Jehovah's Witness organization; the next week like the Seventh-Day Adventists; and, finally, like the Anglo-Israel or British Israel cult.

From the Mormons he can say that, yes, Jesus is God, but only in the sense that *we too* may become gods or be part of the "god family," just as Jesus is. From Seventh-Day Adventism he has borrowed the observance of the seventh-day Sabbath, abstinence from unclean foods (pork, lobster, crab, etc.), and certain methods of prophetic interpretation. From the Dawn Bible Students he lifted the doctrine that Charles Russell taught, namely, that no one is now born again until the Resurrection, Jesus Christ being the sole exception. He also borrowed from the Jehovah's Witnesses the teaching that Satan and all unregenerate men will be annihilated, and that man remains unconscious in the grave until the resurrection. Armstrong also adopts the Jehovah's Witnesses' view of the resurrection of Jesus Christ, and declares that Christ was raised from the dead as a spirit, not as an immortal man with the physical form of flesh and bone. From Anglo-Israelism Armstrong borrowed the teaching that Great Britain and the United States are the ten lost tribes of Israel, which can only be described as a prophetic hallucination discounted by all great scholars of the Hebrew language, of archeology, and of history as without foundation.

It depends, then, on what week you listen to Mr. Armstrong as to what his theological position will be, for he is indeed the cultic chameleon of the airwaves, changing color with the exposition of each borrowed doctrine and then neatly homogenizing all of the parts into a simplistic view of God, the world, the Bible, and the Christian gospel, which is carefully redefined and made palatable to the minds of men unlearned in Armstrong's pronouncements in reference to the historic teachings of the Word of God.

As we shall see when we analyze Mr. Armstrong's theology, it all rests upon his claim that the World Wide Church of God is the only church preaching the same gospel the Lord Jesus Christ preached and that the apostles preached. On this point Mr. Armstrong is adamant:

> I'm going to give you the frank and straightforward answer. You have a right to know all about this great work of God, and about me. First, let me say—this may sound incredible, but it's true—*Jesus Christ foretold this very work—it is, itself, the fulfillment of his prophecy* (Matthew 24:14 and Mark 13:10).

Astounding as it may seem, there is no other work on earth proclaiming to the whole world *this very same gospel* that Jesus taught and proclaimed!

And *listen again!* Read this twice! Realize this, incredible though it may seem—*no other work on earth is proclaiming this true Gospel of Christ to the whole world* as Jesus foretold in Matthew 24:14 and Mark 13:10! This is the most important activity on earth today![2]

The prophecies bring this Church into concrete focus in the 12th chapter of Revelation. There she is shown spiritually, in the glory and splendor of the Spirit of God, but visibly in the world as a persecuted, commandment-keeping Church driven into the wilderness, for 1,260 years, through the middle ages!

In New Testament prophecy *two churches* are described.

One, the great and powerful and universal church, a part of the world, actually ruling in its politics over many nations, and united with "Holy Roman Empire," brought to a concrete focus in Revelation 17.

. . . She is a *mother* Church! Her daughters are also churches who have come out of her, even in protest, calling themselves Protestant—but they are fundamentally of her family in pagan doctrines and practices! They, too, make themselves a part of this world, taking active part in its politics—the very act which made a "whore" out of their Mother!

The entire apostate family—Mother, and more than 500 daughter denominations, all divided against each other and in *confusion* of doctrines, yet all united in the chief pagan doctrines and festivals—has a family *name!* They call themselves "Christian," but God calls them something else—"Mystery, Babylon the Great!"

But the true Church of God is pictured in prophecy as the "Little Flock!" It has kept God's festivals. . . .

That Church always has existed, and it exists today![3]

Yet, is there anything so shocking and so hard to believe as this statement that the whole world is religiously deceived?

Thirty-seven years ago I simply couldn't believe it until I found it proved! And even then, my head was swimming. I found myself all mixed up. To see with my own eyes in the Bible precisely the opposite of what I had

---

[2] Personal letter to Robert Sumner, November 27, 1958.

[3] Easter is Pagan, pp. 8, 9.

been taught from boyhood in Sunday school, well this was pretty hard to take, yet there it was in plain type before my eyes!

If this were the year A.D. 30 and you took a trip to Jerusalem, and there speaking to a throng around him you should see an ordinary looking young man about the age of 33 teaching the same things you hear me and Garner Ted Armstrong say over the radio today, it would have been just as astonishing to you then as it is today—and it was to those who heard Him then. . . . You would have been truly astonished! His doctrine was so different! And He spoke dogmatically with assurance, with power and authority. . . . Yet He had foretold a prophecy. He had foretold wolves coming in sheep's clothing to deceive the world. He had said they would enter in professing to come in His name claiming to be Christian, yet deceiving the whole world. That happened!

For two 19-year time cycles the original apostles did proclaim this Gospel, the Gospel of the Kingdom of God, but in A.D. 69 they fled. In A.D. 70 came the military siege against Jerusalem. The ministers of Satan had wormed their way in, had gained such power that by persecution of political influence they were able to brand the true people of God as heretics and prevent further organized proclaiming of the same Gospel Christ brought from God. For eighteen and one-half centuries that Gospel was not preached. The world was deceived into accepting a false gospel. Today Christ has raised up His work and once again allotted two 19-year time cycles for proclaiming His same Gospel, preparatory to His Second Coming. . . . *The World Tomorrow* and *The Plain Truth* are Christ's instruments which He is powerfully using. Yes, His message is shocking today. Once again it is the voice in the wilderness of religious confusion![4]

"No man ever spoke like this man," reported their officers of the Pharisees regarding Jesus. The multitudes were astonished at His doctrine.

It is the same today, the same living Christ through *The World Tomorrow Broadcast, The Plain Truth Magazine*, and this work proclaims in mighty power around the world the same Gospel preached by Peter, Paul and all the original apostles.[5]

---

[4] *The Inside Story of the World Tomorrow Broadcast*, pp. 7-11.
[5] *Ibid.*, p. 2.

Mr. Armstrong's view of his role, and that of the World Wide Church of God, parallels the claim of all non-Christian cultic leaders, namely, that they are the messenger of God uniquely set apart to either "restore" or to "correctly reinterpret" the Christian message. Charles Russell, founder of Jehovah's Witnesses, maintained that ignorance of his writings could send one into spiritual darkness within two years. Mary Baker Eddy maintained that her discovery of Christian Science was "higher, clearer, and more permanent than that given eighteen centuries ago." Joseph Smith, the Mormon prophet, claimed to be called by God to "restore" the Christian gospel which had been lost for eighteen centuries. And Charles and Myrtle Fillmore were self-appointed messiahs of the Unity School of Christianity's metaphysical maze. The syndrome of self-sanctification runs through the whole kingdom of the cults, and Mr. Armstrong is no exception. We are warned about such self-made "Christs" by Jesus in Matthew 24:24.

But has the World Wide Church of God truly been consistent in its prophetic interpretations and its supernatural pronouncements since Mr. Armstrong first launched it? If Mr. Armstrong and his church really do speak for God, as they maintain, and if it is the only church that is preaching Christ's gospel, we have a right to expect that his church will not deviate from that original gospel; but such is not the case. The following examples of how Mr. Armstrong has changed his position over the last four decades offers ample proof of his fallibility and the emptiness of his claim to divine direction. It is one thing if a man says that he is speaking for himself; it is quite another to represent one's teachings as inspired by God, and as dependable in that most important field of Biblical prophecy. If Mr. Armstrong is preaching Christ's gospel and God's Word, then let him hear what God has said: "I am the Lord; I do not change" (Malachi 3:6). Mr. Armstrong and his church's doctrines, however, *have* changed, and the following evidence is submitted as convincing proof.

The God That Failed[6]

3. Nineteen-year time cycles. In keeping with his almost superstitious fascination with numbers, HWA used to be fond of drawing numerological parallels between the apostolic church and his own organization. Just as nineteen years passed between the Great Day of Pentecost and the penetration of Europe with the Gospel in A.D. 50, so nineteen years passed between the launching of the Armstrong "Work" in 1934 and the Armstrong gospel's "leap" of the Atlantic in 1953, when "The World Tomorrow" was broadcast to Europe via Radio Luxembourg. A second nineteen-year period ended with the destruction of Jerusalem and the flight of the remnant church to Pella in A.D. 69. Although he backed off from setting dates, especially toward the close of the cycle, HWA gave his followers the distinct impression that the "one true church" would be raptured to Petra, in the Jordanian wilderness south of the Dead Sea, and that the dreaded tribulation would commence on the thirty-eighth anniversary of his first regular broadcast, i.e., on January 7, 1972. But as the deadline approached and the endtime events did not materialize, Armstrong withdrew from circulation his booklet *1975 in Prophecy* (which predicted Christ's return in 1975, midway through the seven-year tribulation period), and the doctrines of 1972, Petra, and the nineteen-year time cycles went down the drain.

One does not have to be a great student of either logic or theology to recognize that Mr. Armstrong completely fulfills what Moses had in mind when he spoke of false prophets. In the Book of Deuteronomy, Moses pointed out that one could discover a false prophet by the simple fact that when he spoke in the name of the Lord the things did not come to pass. This is precisely what has occurred with Mr. Armstrong, who claims that his church has been the only voice of God on the earth since 1934. He therefore qualifies under the Mosaic classification, and should not be respected. The god that inspires Mr. Armstrong failed him,

---

[6]*Christianity Today*, Volume XXII, Number 808, April 15, 1977. Personal interview with Garner Ted Armstrong reported by Joseph Martin Hopkins, an authority on the Armstrong cult.

as the evidence shows; he has, therefore, not spoken as a servant of the Lord, nor as a minister of the gospel of Jesus Christ.

BASIC ERRORS IN THEOLOGY

The Trinity

The *purpose of life is that in us* God is really re-creating his *own kind—reproducing himself* after his own kind—for we are, upon real conversion, actually *begotten* as sons (yet unborn) of *God*; then, through study of God's revelation in His Word, living by His very Word, constant prayer, daily experience with trials and testings, we grow spiritually more and more like God, until, at the time of the resurrection we shall be instantaneously *changed* from mortal into *immortal*—we shall then be *born of God*—We *shall then be God!*[7]

. . . I suppose most people think of God as one single individual Person. Or, as a *"trinity." This is not true.*

. . . But the theologians and "Higher Critics" have blindly accepted the heretical and false doctrine introduced by *pagan* false prophets who crept in, that the Holy Spirit is a third person—the heresy of the "trinity." This *limits* God to "Three Persons."[8]

The Deity of Christ

Do you really grasp it? The *purpose* of your being alive is that finally you be *born* into the Kingdom of God, when you will actually *be God*, even as Jesus was and is God, and His Father, a different Person, also is God!

You are setting out on a training to become *creator*—to become *God!*[9]

. . . Yes, and as a *born son of God*, Christ is God! God Almighty His Father is God. They are two separate and individual Persons (see Revelation 5:1, 6,7).[10]

Jesus, *alone*, of all humans, has so far been *saved*! By the resurrective power of *God*! When Jesus comes, at the

---

[7] *Why Were You Born?* pp. 21, 22.
[8] *Just What Do You Mean—Born Again?* pp. 17, 19.
[9] *Why Were You Born?*, p. 22.
[10] *Just What Do You Mean—Born Again?* p. 17.

time of the resurrection of those *in Christ*, He then brings His reward with *Him*![11]

The Resurrection of Christ

. . . When we are *born of God, we shall be* of His *very family*—we shall be *spirit* as He is Spirit—immortal as He is immortal—divine as He is Divine![12]

Jesus Christ was *dead* . . . —but was *revived*!
And the resurrected body was no longer human—it was the Christ resurrected, *immortal*, once again *changed*![13]

. . . If we overcome, grow in grace and knowledge and endure unto the end, *then* . . .
. . . this flesh and blood body shall *become a spirit* body! Then, and not until then, shall we be *fully born of God.*
We are saved by *grace*, and through *faith*—make no mistake about that; *but*—there are conditions!
It is *only* those who, during this Christian, Spirit-begotten life, have grown in knowledge and grace, have overcome, have developed spiritually, done the works of Christ, and endured unto the end, who shall finally be given *immortality*—finally changed from mortal to *immortal* at the time of the Second Coming of Christ (1 Corinthians 15:53-54).[14]

All true Christians who shall have died before Christ's coming shall rise first—in a resurrection—and then all Christians *still alive*, in mortal flesh, shall be instantaneously—in the twinkling of an eye—*changed from mortal to immortal*—from material flesh to immaterial spirit—from *human* to *divine*, at last *born of God*![15]

We are now *flesh*—vile, corruptible flesh subject to rotting and decay. But at Christ's coming, when we shall be *born of God*, this vile body shall be *changed*, and made exactly like Jesus in His *glorified body*.[16]

---

[11] *Why Were You Born?* p. 11.
[12] *Just What Do You Mean—Born Again?* p. 17
[13] *The Plain Truth*, April, 1963, p. 10.
[14] *All About Water Baptism*, pp. 1 and 3.
[15] *Just What Do You Mean—Born Again?* p. 13.
[16] *Ibid.*, p. 15.

The New Birth

But, He was then *born of God, how?* By a resurrection from the dead (Romans 1:4). When ? *At the time* of His resurrection!

And *that is* the way *you* and I shall look, if and when we are finally *born of God!* These deceived people who talk about having had a "born again experience" certainly don't look like *that!*

That tremendous, glorious event of being *born of God* is to take place *at the resurrection of the just*—at the time of Christ's Second Coming to earth![17]

Salvation by Grace

Salvation, then, is a *process!*

But how the god of this world would blind your eyes to that! He tries to deceive you into thinking all there is to it is just "accepting Christ" with "*no works*"—and presto-chango, you are pronounced "Saved."

But the *Bible* reveals that *none* is yet "saved."[18]

People have been taught, falsely, that "Christ *completed* the plan of salvation on the Cross"—when actually it was only *begun* there. The popular denominations have taught, "Just believe—that's all there is to it; believe on the Lord Jesus Christ, and you are that instant *saved!*"

That teaching is false! And because of deception—because the *true Gospel* of Jesus Christ has been blotted out, lo these 1900 years by the preaching of a false gospel *about the person* of Christ—and often a false Christ at that—millions today *worship Christ*—and all in vain!

The *blood* of Christ does not finally save any man. The death of Christ merely paid the penalty of sin in our stead—it wipes the slate clean of past sins—it saves us merely from the *death penalty*—it removes that which separated us from God and reconciles us to God.[19]

. . . So it is not only *possible* but *obligatory*—that we obey God's spiritual law, the *ten commandments*, as they are magnified throughout the Bible. Keeping them in the spirit does *not mean* "spiritualizing" them away.

. . . But by exercising the *will* to always obey God, and

[17] *Ibid.*, pp. 13-15.
[18] *Why Were You Born?* p. 11.
[19] *All About Water Baptism*, pp. 1, 2.

by receiving the extra help He needed to Master His fleshly desires, Jesus *repudiated* the sway of sin of the human flesh and showed that the law of God *could be kept.*[20]

Legalism, the Sabbath, and Unclean Foods

Passover, the days of unleavened bread, Pentecost, and the holy days God had ordained *forever* were all observed by Jesus. . . .

The New Testament reveals that Jesus, the apostles, and the New Testament Church, both Jewish and Gentile-born, observed God's Sabbath, and God's festivals—weekly and annually.[21]

It would be impossible in the light of the above and the limitations of space to answer all of Mr. Armstrong's mistakes in detail, but a Biblical critique is vitally important if Christians are to protect themselves from the subtleties of his legalistic errors as well as to evangelize those within the Armstrong movement who are sincere but deceived. There is also a great mass of persons subjected to constant bombardment of Armstrong theology through the media who need to be warned that they are dealing with a theological wolf garbed in the clothing of an innocent lamb. Warning and exhortation are never popular in any age, but the church has the task of doing both, and the facts must be presented and carefully weighed in the interest of truth.

TO EVERY MAN AN ANSWER

In the very beginning of the survey of the World Wide Church of God I pointed out that Mr. Armstrong draws his theology from many sources, and then sprays on it a light veneer of Christian terminology combined with out-of-context quotations from the Bible. This tends to confuse people, many of whom are desperately seeking for truth and for some word from God to meet their needs. In the

---

[20] *The Plain Truth Magazine*, November, 1963, pp. 11, 12.
[21] *Easter Is Pagan*, pp. 4, 12.

midst of all this are pious pronouncements from Garner Ted, such as "Don't take my word for it—check it with the Bible." I intend to do just that now, and to find out if the Armstrong theology will stand up under the test of Biblical revelation.

The Trinity

The World Wide Church of God, as the preceding quotes reveal, rejects the Christian doctrine of the Trinity, teaching instead that the Trinity, or God's nature, is not limited to three Persons, but that actually the Trinity is a family concept in which all persons who accept Mr. Armstrong's religion will share! The Mormon Church has taught for more than 140 years that through their Priesthood a man may become *a god*, but Mr. Armstrong has surpassed them in that man may *become God*.

Biblical theology is most clear at this point, teaching that within the nature of the one eternal God there are three Persons—the Father, the Son, and the Holy Spirit (2 Peter 1:17; Exodus 3:14; Revelation 1:11-18; John 1:1, 18; 8:58; Revelation 22:12-16; Colossians 2:9; Titus 2:13; Acts 5:3, 4; Isaiah 48:16; 45:22). The Lord Jesus Christ commanded that the gospel be preached in all the world and that baptism be administered in the name of the Trinity, i.e., God (Matthew 28:19). Far from teaching that man may become God, the Scriptures teach that God forbids any such idea (Isaiah 43:10), affirming instead that God is unique and one in essence (Deuteronomy 6:4).

It is unnecessary to go any further into a refutation of Mr. Armstrong's views on the Trinity, since it has been documented from both Scripture and history that the Christian church has always taught unity in Trinity and Trinity in unity, the full understanding of which God has reserved to Himself until the day when Christ will deliver up the kingdom to the Father, and God will be all in all (1 Corinthians 15:28).

For further study and confirmation, consult the following texts:

1. Old Testament Hints—Genesis 1:26; 3:22; 11:7; Isaiah 6:8; 48:12; Zechariah 12:12:9, 10.
2. The Creation—Genesis 1:2; John 1·3
3. The Incarnation—Luke 1:35.
4. The Baptism of Christ—Matthew 3:16, 17.
5. The Resurrection of Christ—Acts 3:26; 1 Thessalonians 1:10 (the Father); John 2:19-21 (the Son); Romans 8:11; 1 Peter 3:18 (the Holy Spirit); Acts 17:31 (God).
6. The Great Commission—Matthew 28:19.
7. The Divine Benediction—2 Corinthians 13:14. See also John 14:16, 26; 15:26.

The Deity of Christ

Perhaps the most famous of Garner Ted Armstrong's sermons, which has been re-broadcast many times on television and radio, deals with the identity of Jesus Christ. In this lengthy exposition, Garner Ted Armstrong affirms that "Jesus is God," thus creating the impression that the Armstrong religion believes in the deity of Jesus Christ. As we have observed from his own published statements, Garner Armstrong and his father deny the unique deity of Jesus Christ, affirming that we can become God "just as Jesus is God . . . and His Father is God. . . ." New Testament theology specifically contradicts the Armstrongs at this point by declaring that Jesus Christ is Deity from all eternity (Revelation 1:7, 8; John 1:1; Colossians 2:9), whereas *man* is created in time and does not have an eternal past. For us to be God as Jesus is God, we would have to be eternal—but we are not (Genesis 1:26, 27; 3:19, 22).

Even to Old Testament scholars the deity of the Savior was no secret, since he was termed by Isaiah "the father of eternity" (Isaiah 9:6), whose heritage is "from eternity" (Micah 5:2). In direct confrontation with the Jews of His day who were hostile to His messianic claims, Christ asserted the divine Name as belonging to Him (John 8:58), and the Jews, understanding this claim, sought to stone Him for it (verse 59). Throughout His earthly ministry Jesus Christ accepted worship (Matthew 8:2; 14:33; John 9:35-39; 20:27-29) and allowed Thomas to proclaim Him the eternal God (John 20:28). In his Epistle to the Colossians, Paul describes Christ as the Creator of all things (1:16), and in Philippians chapter 2 it is declared that He never ceased to be in the form of God (verse 6). Who can read the first chapter of the Epistle to the Hebrews without recognizing that Christ is the visible stamp of the divine nature in human flesh (verse 3), as well as the only one ever to be addressed by the Father, "Thy throne, O God, is forever and ever" (verse 8). The genuine deity of Jesus Christ is the church's first affirmation—"He is Lord of all." God literally became flesh for us and our salvation (John 1:1, 14). Mr. Armstrong's error is the same error as that of the Sadducees, of whom Christ said, "You do err, not understanding the Scriptures nor the power of God" (Mark 12:24).

The Resurrection of Christ

The Apostle Paul in his First Epistle to the Corinthians, chapter 15, adamantly and dogmatically taught that "if Christ be not risen from the dead your faith is empty; you are still in your sins" (verse 17).

Even a superficial reading of any Greek lexicon or dictionary would have told Mr. Armstrong that the word "resurrection" refers to the body, never to the soul or spirit, and this holds true in the Hebrew language as well. When the Apostle was speaking, then, for him the term "risen," the concept of the resurrection itself, involved the body and not the spirit. By teaching that Jesus Christ rose from the dead as a spirit without a physical form, Mr. Armstrong joins the Jehovah's Witnesses, the Dawn Bible Students, and countless liberal clergymen in the promulgation of an error first made by the disciples of our Lord, and corrected personally by Him! Luke informs us that Christ's disciples believed He was a spirit when they first saw Him after His resurrection, to which misconception Jesus responded:

> They were startled and frightened, thinking they saw a ghost. He said to them, "Why are you troubled, and why do doubts rise in your minds? Look at my hands and my feet. It is I myself! Touch me and see; a ghost does not have flesh and bones, as you see I have" (Luke 24:37-39 NIV).

Mr. Armstrong stands contradicted out of the mouth of our Lord Himself, not to mention Luke and John. In the twentieth chapter of John's Gospel, Christ again affirmed the bodily nature of His resurrection (verses 24-28), and in the one prophecy He gave concerning the nature of His resurrection body He vigorously affirmed it to be physical (John 2:19-21).

The final blow to the Armstrong myth that Christ was raised as a spirit is found in 1 John 3:2, where Christians are told that "it does not yet appear what we shall be, but we know that when he appears we shall be like him, for we shall see him as he is."

It is obvious from 1 Thessalonians chapter 4 that man emerges from the resurrection with a *physical form*, and that even in the resurrection of the unjust, they too will have physical forms (1 Thessalonians 4:13-17; Revelation 20:11-15).

Logic compels me to point out that if we are going to be like Christ in the resurrection and we are to receive resurrection bodies similar to His, He could hardly have been raised a spirit.

Since all hope for the Christian is grounded in the resurrection of the Lord Jesus, Mr. Armstrong with his denial of that resurrection attacks the cornerstone of the Christian faith, a faith he claims to support. Jesus said, "Wisdom is justified of her children." Let the wise student of Scripture understand that when Mr. Armstrong speaks of the resurrection of Christ, *his* Christ is a ghost; the *real* Jesus is a resurrected, immortal man.

The New Birth—A New Twist

The doctrine of the new birth or spiritual regeneration as it is taught in the New Testament apparently has an effect upon Mr. Armstrong which is little short of hysterical. In his pamphlet *Just What Do You Mean—Born Again?* he vigorously criticizes the Christian doctrine of regeneration (see preceding quotations on this subject), and in its place he substitutes what is by all odds one of the strangest doctrines in cultism. Through it he has quite literally given the new birth a new twist!

According to the theology of The World Wide Church of God, the doctrine of the new birth is divided into two areas. In the first, which takes place upon the acceptance of Jesus Christ as the Son of God, the believer is impregnated with the life of God through the Holy Spirit, which Armstrong terms "begetting." The second phase is the new birth itself, which, he informs us, takes place not at the moment of faith but at the resurrection of the body![22]

Mr. Armstrong strenuously maintains that it is "a universal error" to believe that when a person is converted. when he has fully repented and accepted Christ in faith, such a person is born again in the Biblical sense. For Herbert Armstrong the original Greek word *gennao* is the pivot point of the controversy. Armstrong holds that, since the word can also be translated "beget" or "conceive," the translators of the Bible erred in not rendering the word consistently as "begotten" instead of "born," and this they did because "they did not themselves understand God's plan. . . . The experience of conversion in this life is a begettal, a conception, an impregnation, but not yet a birth."[23]

It is worthwhile to note in studying this particular phase of Mr. Armstrong's theology that his appeal to the Greek, which was meant to carry the convincing weight of scholastic authority, in reality becomes the proverbial

---

[22] *Just What Do You Mean—Born Again?* pp. 6, 7.
[23] *Ibid.*, pp. 7, 8.

albatross around his neck. Mr. Armstrong's contention that "the original Greek in which the New Testament was written has only the one word for both meanings"[24] is a most damaging remark, for any good lexicon reveals immediately that the Greek has at least four other terms to describe the idea of conception and birth (*sullabousa, tiktei, apotelestheisa,* and *apokuei*), which are translated variously as "conceive," "bring forth," "delivered," "born," "when finished," and "begat." One need only study Luke 1:24, 37; 2:21, 36; James 1:15, 18 and numerous other passages, and he will come to the immediate conclusion that Mr. Armstrong has no concept whatever of New Testament Greek. In fact, the Greek language even has a term which describes pregnancy from conception to delivery!

The followers of Mr. Armstrong must settle for an impregnation by the Spirit and a gestation period (their entire life!) before they can be born again. This new birth is dependent upon keeping the commandments of God and enduring to the end (in Mr. Armstrong's theology), a fact overlooked by some of his more zealous disciples.

The fact that the new birth has nothing to do with the resurrection is demonstrated by the usage of the term by the Apostle Peter, who reminds us that through faith in the Lord Jesus Christ we have been "born again" (past tense) "not of corruptible seed, but of incorruptible, by the Word of God which liveth and abideth forever" (1 Peter 1:23).

The new birth in the New Testament is synonymous with spiritual regeneration to eternal life, and the very fact that Jesus Christ and the apostles described the possessors of the new birth as "saved" decimated Mr. Armstrong's contention that one must wait until the resurrection in order to be born again.

In his Epistle to the Ephesians the Apostle Paul is adamant in his declaration that "by grace you have been

---

[24] *Ibid.,* p. 7.

saved through faith; and this is not your own doing, it is the gift of God—not because of works, lest anyone should boast" (Ephesians 2:8, literal translation). Here is the usage of the past tense in reference to Christians, an instance which is amply supplemented throughout the New Testament by such passages as John 5:24; 3:36; 6:47; Romans 8:1; 1 Peter 1:18; 1 John 5:1, 11-13; 20.

Mr. Armstrong has no scholarly precedent for subdividing the new birth and attempting to attach it to the resurrection of the body, something which the Scripture nowhere does. His is a lame attempt to distort the basic meaning of *gennao* (which, incidentally, he himself admits is listed in the lexicon as "to be born, to bring forth, to be delivered of"). It is only one more indication of the limitations of his resources.

After reading Mr. Armstrong's statements, any serious student of the Bible wonders how anyone could take seriously his theological interpretations, for if there is one thing that the Bible *does* emphatically teach, it is the fact that salvation is *not* a process but an accomplished fact, based upon the *completed* sacrifice of Jesus Christ (Hebrews 1:3; 9:26, 28).

Regarding Mr. Armstrong's shocking statement to the effect that the blood of Christ does not finally save anyone, this is in direct contradiction to the words of the Apostle Peter, who taught that persons have not been redeemed by anything corruptible but "by the precious blood of Christ" (1 Peter 1:19). It should be noted that this is in the *past tense* as an accomplished fact, a teaching amplified in the Book of Hebrews repeatedly. The writer of Hebrews tells us that "by one offering He has perfected forever them that are sanctified" and that by the will of God "we are sanctified through the offering of the body of Jesus Christ once for all" (Hebrews 10:14, 20).

The Lord Jesus has entered

> ..not into a sanctuary made with hands, a copy of the true one, but into heaven itself, now to appear in the

presence of God on our behalf. . . . But as it is, he has
appeared once for all at the end of the age to put away sin
by the sacrifice of himself. And just as it is appointed for
men to die once, and after that comes the judgment, so
Christ, having been offered once to bear the sins of many,
will appear a second time, not to deal with sin but to save
those who are eagerly waiting for him (Hebrews 9:24, 26-
28 RSV).

When Jesus Christ addressed Nicodemus (John 3) and
spoke of the new birth, He connected this birth to the
Person of the Holy Spirit, whom the disciples received in
the upper room (John 20) and whose power and presence
were manifested at Pentecost (Acts 2). This has always been
accepted in Christian theology for just what the Bible says it
is—an instantaneous experience of spiritual cleansing and
re-creation synonymous with the exercise of saving faith in
the Person of Jesus Christ and through the agency of the
grace of God (Acts 16:31; 2:8-10; Colossians 1:13, 14;
Galatians 2:20; 1 Corinthians 6:11, 19; 2 Corinthians 5:17).

The Apostle Paul instructs us that our salvation has been
accomplished not by any efforts on our part, but by "the
kindness and love of God our Savior" (Titus 3:4-7). It is not
something we must wait for until the resurrection; it is our
present possession in Christ, totally separate from the immortality of the body, which is to be bestowed at the return
of Christ and the resurrection of the body (1 Corinthians
15:49-54; 1 John 3:2; Romans 6:5).

It is all well and good if Mr. Armstrong's followers wish
to make the new birth a process, as indeed they do with the
doctrine of salvation, but we must be quick to point out that
this is not the *Christian* doctrine of the new birth and is not
consistent with the revelation of the Bible. Mr. Armstrong's
new twist to the new birth is just that, and the Christian
church can ill afford to sit by in silence while The World
Wide Church of God propagates it as Biblical theology.

Salvation by Grace

As the theology of Armstrongism does violence to the

true nature of the new birth, so also does it categorically deny the Biblical doctrine of the atonement.

According to Mr. Armstrong:

> Salvation, then, is a *process*! But how the god of this world would blind your eyes to that! He tries to deceive you into thinking all there is to it is just "accepting Christ" with "*no works*," and presto changeover, you are pronounced "Saved!" . . . But the *Bible* reveals that *none* is as yet "saved." . . . People have been taught, falsely, that "Christ completed the plan of salvation on the Cross"—when actually it was only *begun* there. The popular denominations have taught "Just believe, that's all there is to it; believe on the Lord Jesus Christ and you are that instant *saved*." That teaching is false. . . . The *blood* of Christ does not finally save any man. . . .[25]

Mr. Armstrong and his World Wide Church of God consistently ignore the fact that

> Christ had offered for all time a single sacrifice for sins. . . . Therefore, brethren, since we have confidence to enter the sanctuary by the blood of Jesus, by the new and living way which he opened for us through the curtain, that is, through his flesh, and since we have a great priest over the house of God, let us draw near with a true heart in full assurance of faith, with our hearts sprinkled clean from an evil conscience and our bodies washed with pure water. Let us hold fast the confession of our hope without wavering, for he who promised is faithful (Hebrews 10:12, 19-23 RSV).

The Apostle Paul reiterates the completed nature of the atonement upon the cross when he deals with the subject in such passages as Ephesians 1:7, Colossians 1:20, and Romans 5:9. The Apostle John's reminder that God has provided for continual cleansing from sin (1 John 1:7, 9) should only serve to strengthen Christians in the knowledge that Jesus Christ has indeed by the sacrifice of the cross "loosed us from our sins in His own blood" (Revelation 1:5, literal translation). This is a completed act, the benefits

---

[25] *Why Were You Born?* p. 11; *All About Water Baptism*, pp. 1, 2, 3, 8.

of which are shed abroad in the hearts of all true believers by the Holy Spirit. Nowhere does the Bible teach that the atonement of Christ is *yet* to be completed! This particular doctrine is drawn from the early writings of Seventh-Day Adventists, with whom, as we mentioned, Mr. Armstrong was associated at one time. It is to the credit of the Adventists that their denomination has officially repudiated this position, maintaining that the atonement has already been completed.

Pauline theology makes clear the fact that in Jesus Christ God has determined to redeem men by sovereign grace, and the record still stands:

> For what saith the scripture? Abraham believed God, and it was counted unto him for righteousness. Now to him that worketh is the reward not reckoned of grace, but of debt. But to him that worketh not, but believeth on him that justifieth the ungodly, his faith is counted for righteousness. Even as David also describeth the blessedness of the man unto whom God imputeth righteousness without works, saying, blessed are they whose iniquities are forgiven, and whose sins are covered. Blessed is the man to whom the Lord will not impute sin (Romans 4:3-8 KJV).

The theology of the World Wide Church of God in regard to the doctrine of salvation is refuted thoroughly by the Apostle Paul in his Epistle to the Galatians; when describing the purpose of the law of God, Paul points out that its primary function was to "lead us to Christ" that we might be justified by faith. The law was a pedagogue, a teacher, but it was finally and completely fulfilled in the Person of Jesus Christ, who was incarnate love, as the universal, all-fulfilling principle which is implemented through grace, first toward God and then toward one's neighbor (see Romans 13:8-11).

Mr. Armstrong attaches to salvation the requirement of "keeping the law and commandments of God." This can only be described as adding to the gospel of grace the condition of law-keeping, a first-century heresy scathingly denounced in the Galatian Epistle as "another gospel" by no less an authority on the law than the Apostle Paul himself (Galatians 2:16, 21; 1:8, 9).

If all law is fulfilled in love, as Christ and the apostles taught, then the insistence upon observance of the Ten Commandments (or, for that matter, the other six hundred laws of Moses) on the part of Mr. Armstrong and his followers as a condition of salvation injects into the Christian church what the apostles so successfully expelled (Matthew 22:36-40; Acts 15:24).

It is certainly true that no informed Christian believes in the destruction or setting aside of the laws of God, but, as we shall see, when dealing with the Seventh-Day Adventists' conception of this subject, there is a vast difference between the *abolition* of law and the *fulfillment* of law, which fulfillment Christ accomplished once for all on the cross (Romans 3:31, 10:4).

Legalism, the Sabbath, and Unclean Foods

Inherent within the theological structure of The World Wide Church of God, and stemming from Mr. Armstrong's perversion of the Biblical doctrine of salvation, is his insistence (also borrowed from the Seventh-Day Adventists) that Christians abstain from specific types of food which he claims are "unclean."

No devoted follower of The World Wide Church of God will therefore eat pork, lobster, clams, shrimp, oysters, or any of the other prohibitions of the Mosaic system. They are, in effect, Orthodox Jews in this particular area of theology!

In his First Epistle to Timothy, the Apostle Paul recognized among the Gentiles the problem of so-called unclean foods and dealt with it in the following manner:

> Now the Spirit expressly says that in later times some will depart from the faith by giving heed to deceitful spirits and doctrines of demons, through the pretensions of liars whose consciences are seared, who forbid

marriage and enjoin abstinence from foods which God created to be received with thanksgiving by those who believe and know the truth. For everything created by God is good, and nothing is to be rejected if it is received with thanksgiving; for then it is consecrated by the word of God and prayer (1 Timothy 4:1-5 RSV).

Further comment on this particular subject is unnecessary in the light of the Apostle's clear statement, but a reading of the fourteenth chapter of Romans reveals instantly that Christians are not to sit in judgment upon one another regarding days of worship of foods to be consumed. We are not to judge spirituality on the basis of diet or the observance of days. But in The World Wide Church of God this is not true, for Mr. Armstrong does indeed sit in judgment upon all those who do not subscribe to his particular interpretation of dietary laws allegedly enforceable in this era of history.

Relative to the problem of Sabbath-keeping, Mr. Armstrong also derived this from the Seventh-Day Adventist denomination, but he has gone further than the Adventists have ever even intimated.

The literature of The World Wide Church of God insists upon the observance of the Jewish feast days, new moons, festivals, and sabbaths, all of which were dealt with fully and finally by the Apostle Paul in his Colossian Epistle:

And you, who were dead in trespasses and the uncircumcision of your flesh, God made alive together with him, having forgiven us all our trespasses, having cancelled the bond which stood against us with its legal demands; this he set aside, nailing it to the cross. He disarmed the principalities and powers and made a public example of them, triumphing over them in him.

Therefore let no one pass judgment on you in questions of food and drink or with regard to a festival or a new moon or a sabbath. These are only a shadow of what is to come; but the substance belongs to Christ (Colossians 2:13-17 RSV).

When the preceding quotation from Paul is placed beside his counsel in Romans 14, the picture is transparently clear:

> Let not him who eats despise him who abstains, and let
> not him who abstains pass judgment on him who eats; for
> God has welcomed him. Who are you to pass judgment
> on the servant of another? It is before his own master that
> he stands or falls. And he will be upheld, for the Master is
> able to make him stand.
>
> One man esteems one day as better than another, while
> another man esteems all days alike. Let everyone be fully
> convinced in his own mind. He who observes the day
> observes it in honor of the Lord. He also who eats, eats in
> honor of the Lord, since he gives thanks to God, while he
> who abstains, abstains in honor of the Lord and gives
> thanks to God. . . . Why do you pass judgment on your
> brother? Or you, why do you despise your
> brother? . . . Then let us no more pass judgment on one
> another, but rather decide never to put a stumbling-block
> or hindrance in the way of a brother. I know and am
> persuaded in the Lord Jesus that nothing is unclean in
> itself; but it is unclean for anyone who thinks it un-
> clean. . . . Do not, for the sake of food, destroy the work
> of God. Everything is indeed clean, but it is wrong for
> anyone to make others fall by what he eats; it is right not
> to eat meat or drink wine or do anything that makes your
> brother stumble (Romans 14:3-6, 10, 13, 14, 20, 21 RSV).

There is a memorable passage in the Book of Acts
where, when the Council of Jerusalem was in session concerning the problem of Jewish prohibitions on diet and
practice as it affected the Gentile converts, the Apostle
James once for all time dealt with the issue, a fact Mr.
Armstrong seems content to ignore:

> Wherefore my sentence is that we trouble not them
> which from among the Gentiles are turned to God, but
> that we write unto them that they abstain from pollutions
> of idols, and from fornication, and from things strangled,
> and from blood. . . . Forasmuch as we have heard that
> certain which went out from us have troubled you with
> words, subverting your souls, saying that ye must be
> circumcised and keep the law, to whom we gave no such
> commandment. . . . For it seemed good to the Holy
> Ghost and to us to lay upon you no greater burden than
> these necessary things: that ye abstain from meats offered
> to idols, and from blood, and from things strangled, and
> from fornication, from which, if ye keep yourselves, ye
> shall do well (Acts 15:19, 20, 24, 28, 29 KJV).

It is evident that law-keeping, dietary prohibitions, the Mosaic ordinances which were binding upon Israel, and the Jewish customs of observances of feasts, etc., were abrogated by the Holy Spirit (verse 28), and it is certainly not amiss to comment that what the Spirit of God saw fit to lift as restrictions upon the church of Jesus Christ, the so-called World Wide Church of God has no right to reimpose! Mr. Armstrong, however, has done precisely this, and his action stands condemned not only by the Council at Jerusalem and the Apostle James, but by the clear words of the Apostle Paul and the pronouncement of the Holy Spirit Himself.

From our survey of the World Wide Church of God it is apparent that the errors of Mr. Armstrong's religion place him well outside the pale of historic Christianity, and very definitely within the category of non-Christian cultism.

There are many sincere and devoted truth-seekers within the Armstrong cult, many of whom have been gleaned from liberal Protestantism and Catholicism, and who are attracted by Mr. Armstrong's emphasis upon the Bible, perverted though it may be. I have no doubt that there are people within the structure of the Armstrong religion who have a simple faith in Jesus Christ from their past experience and have simply been confused by Armstrong's dogmatic pronouncements in the name of God. The Apostle Paul told us of such persons in need of reclamation in 2 Corinthians 11:3, 4:

> But I am afraid that just as Eve was deceived by the serpent's cunning, your minds may somehow be led astray from your sincere and pure devotion to Christ. For if someone comes to you and preaches a Jesus other than the Jesus we preached, or if you receive a different spirit from the one you received, or a different gospel from the one you accepted, you put up with it easily enough (2 Corinthians 11:3, 4 NIV).

Let us take the words of the Apostle seriously, believing that the followers of Mr. Armstrong have indeed been deceived by a counterfeit Christ, a counterfeit Holy Spirit, and a counterfeit gospel; and let us reach out to them, answering their questions and extending the love of Christ, so that they may "be reconciled to God" (2 Corinthians 5:20). This is the task of the church; this is the only effective answer to the rise of the cults.

Four

THE MORMON MAZE

Of all the major cults extant in the melting pot of religions called American, none is more subtle or dangerous to the unwary soul than The Church of Jesus Christ of Latter-day Saints, the official name for Mormonism. This stalwart organization is composed of approximately 3.5 million members, all active in zealously promoting the "revelations" of "Prophet" Joseph Smith and the indomitable Brigham Young. Ruled by a first president and a supreme council ironically titled "The Twelve Apostles," the Mormon religion stretches the length and breadth of our country and reaches even to numerous foreign mission fields throughout the world. Indeed, with its tremendous wealth, growing prestige, and zeal for missionary programs, Mormonism constitutes an immense threat to the church of Jesus Christ of our era.

HISTORICAL VIEW

From Salt Lake City, Utah, the hub of the Mormon wheel of ever-expanding influence, 18,600 energetic Mormon missionaries travel each year two-by-two, even as the apostles of old,[1] in order to carry one of the cleverest counterfeits of the true gospel yet devised, one which stands ready to ensnare the souls of a world rich in religion and bankrupt in the faith that saves. Today Mormonism is powerful, its missionary program immense, and its inroads upon the Christian faith tragic. But what type of doctrine is

---

[1] Jehovah's Witnesses also follow this practice when possible.

it that appeals so much to the modern mind that orthodox Christianity suffers as a result? Who brought about this Mormon religion which today plagues our mission fields? What do Mormons believe, and how can they be effectively evangelized and their influence combatted? These questions are being asked by concerned Christian pastors, evangelists, and laymen everywhere as they recognize the threat of Mormonism and the need for a definite plan of action to meet the growing challenge at home and abroad. Let us therefore examine the history and doctrines of this "new gospel," which found its origin not in the inspired writings of the New Testament but in the mind of one Joseph Smith, Jr., in the year 1830.

THE MORMON PROPHET

Joseph Smith, Jr., founder of the Mormon religion, was born in Royalton, Vermont, on December 23, 1805. He was the son of a poverty-stricken, part-time treasure hunter who spent his time dabbling in the occult and searching for Captain Kidd's treasure.[2] Young "Joe," as he was irreverently referred to in his pre-prophet days, early gained the reputation of being the biggest faker of the entire Smith family, and was engaged for the most part of his youth in seeking Captain Kidd's treasure and in gazing through "peep stones" in which, he declared to superstitious neighbors, he could see their futures. This charge, long debated, was recently validated by an articulate historian, Rev. Wesley P. Walters. While in Norwich, New York, Rev. Walters searched through the Chenango County's "dead storage" and, on July 28, 1971, uncovered the justice's and constable's bills of an 1826 trial in which Joseph Smith, Jr. was labeled "the glass looker," and was convicted for this misdemeanor, resulting in a small fine. A personal account from Pomeroy Tucker, a man who was

---

[2] Wm. Alexander Linn, *The Story of the Mormons* (New York: Macmillan Co., 1902), p. 10.

personally acquainted with the Smith family, can best portray the early character of Joseph Smith. Witness his unprejudiced testimony:

> At this period in the life and career of Joseph Smith, Jr., or 'Joe Smith,' as he was universally named, and the Smith family, they were popularly regarded as an illiterate, whiskey-drinking, shiftless, irreligious race of people—the first named, the chief subject of this biography, being unanimously voted the laziest and most worthless of the generation. From the age of twelve to twenty years he is distinctly remembered as a dull-eyed, flaxen-haired, prevaricating boy—noted only for his indolent and vagabondish character, and his habits of exaggeration and untruthfulness. Taciturnity was among his characteristic idiosyncrasies, and he seldom spoke to anyone outside of his intimate associates, except when first addressed by another; and then, by reason of the extravagances of his statement, his word was received with the least confidence by those who knew him best. He could utter the most palpable exaggeration or marvelous absurdity with the utmost apparent gravity.[3]

Further than this, the following testimony was given by prominent members of the community in which the Smith family lived:

> We, the undersigned, being personally acquainted with the family of Joseph Smith, Sr., with whom the Gold Bible, so-called, originated, state: That they were not only a lazy, indolent set of men, but also intemperate, and their word was not to be depended upon; and that we are truly glad to dispense with their society.
>
> We, the undersigned, have been acquainted with the Smith family for a number of years, while they resided near this place, and we have no hesitation in saying that we consider them destitute of that moral character which ought to entitle them to the confidence of any community. They were particularly famous for visionary projects; spent much of their time in digging for money which they pretended was hid in the earth, not far from their residence, where they used to spend their time in

---

[3] Pomeroy Tucker, *Origin, Rise and Progress of Mormonism*, (New York, 1847), p. 16.

digging for hidden treasures. Joseph Smith, Sr., and his son Joseph were, in particular, considered entirely destitute of moral character, and addicted to vicious habits.[4]

This is a far different picture from that so vividly manufactured by numerous Mormon historians. It should be noted that this is contemporary evidence, not the product of flowery Mormon historians who have distorted the true character of Smith and portrayed him as a noble, self-sacrificing youth dedicated to the gospel of Christ and the Bible, which history tells us he emphatically was not!

THE MORMON REVELATION

The general story of how Smith received his "revelation" is a most genuine piece of fantasy and would be occasion for genuine laughter were it not for the tragic fact that almost 3.5 million people believe it as divine truth. As the story goes, young Smith, bent on serving the true God, was the recipient of a vision in which both the Father and the Son spoke to him, despaired of the failure of Christendom to dispense the gospel, and anointed the humble Joseph "Prophet of the Restored Christian Religion."[5] Accompanying these celestial manifestations, young Smith was in the course of time interviewed by a most obliging angel, Moroni by name, who entrusted to the fledgling prophet the privilege of translating the "Golden Plates" of what later became the fabulous *Book of Mormon*,[6] which was among other things a dismal plagiarism of the King James Bible. The thoughtful angel also provided the illiterate Smith with a pair of miraculous spectacles, Urim and Thummim respectively, with the aid of which Joe "translated" the Golden Plates for posterity. Smith's cohort

---

[4] Ibid, p. 10.

[5] Tract published by The Church of Jesus Christ of Latter-day Saints, quoted from *The Examiner*, January, 1952, pp. 21, 22.

[6] J.K. Van Baalen, *The Chaos of Cults*, pp. 144, 145.

in the preparation of this gigantic hoax was one Martin Harris, by turn a former Quaker, Universalist, Baptist, Presbyterian, and religious adventurer whose sanity, it was said by contemporaries, would have been hard to establish in a court of law.

Various Mormon historians have striven vainly to establish the veracity of *The Book of Mormon*, which along with *The Pearl of Great Price* and *Doctrine and Covenants* makes up the central written authority of the Mormon faith.[7] But the weight of evidence is far too great for history to allow this sham to be cloaked in the finery of saintly language and masqueraded as divine revelation. *The Book of Mormon* contains literally hundreds of readings lifted almost bodily from the King James Bible, and it repeatedly reveals the linguistic shortcomings of the "Prophet" Smith. It should be noted, incidentally, that *The Book of Mormon* supposedly antedates the King James Bible by many, many centuries; yet in numerous places the readings from it are identical with the English version.

These accounts are not idle gossip or empty accusations; they are simply a matter of cold hard facts. Joseph Smith was a notoriously immoral man who openly practiced polygamy at the Mormon Sodom, Nauvoo, Illinois, and dared to maintain to his legal wife Emma that Almighty God approved his adulterous activities. The "Prophet," as he was universally acclaimed by the faithful, met a violent and it may be said unjust death at the hands of an irate mob who stormed the jail in which he was imprisoned awaiting trial and shot both him and his brother Hyrum to death in a particularly brutal miscarriage of justice. This was a doubly unfortunate event since it had the undesired effect of thrusting martyrdom upon the "Prophet" and thus plant-

---

[7] All three books have received literally thousands of changes. The latter two are sometimes almost unrecognizable in parts when compared with the originals. We have maintained for many years that Rev. Solomon Spalding and *not* Joseph Smith authored the *Book of Mormon*.

ed the seeds of what today has become the Mormon Church.

PROPHET YOUNG

Upon the death of Joseph Smith, Brigham Young, devoted disciple of the "Prophet," grasped the helm of the faltering Mormon bark and steered a straight course westward, bound on finding a place where the followers of the "new revelation" might settle peacefully, unhampered by the great mass of mankind who believed that one wife is enough for any home and that the gospel of Jesus Christ was sufficiently plain without "Prophet" Smith's "revelations" to "explain" it. The Mormons finally settled near what is now Salt Lake City, Utah, and founded a small, extremely powerful kingdom ruled by Young and the "Twelve Apostles," whose word was life and death to those who chose the Mormon religion. In this little kingdom polygamy flourished openly, and it was only at the turn of the century that this unchristian practice was outlawed. Despite the enforcement of the law, however, there are still some segments of Mormon origin, misnamed "Fundamentalists," who have as late as 1975 been arrested for practicing polygamy.

Today the Mormons occupy a position of great prestige. Strangely enough, one of the vaunted "Twelve Apostles" is a former member of the Presidential Cabinet, ex-Secretary of Agriculture Ezra Taft Benson. Mormons are considered by many to be "Fundamentalists," and sad to say zealous Mormon missionaries quote the Bible far more freely than many true Christians whose task it is to win the followers of Joseph Smith to Jesus Christ. This is a calling which the Christian church has badly neglected, to which fact the rise of Mormonism and its great threat to evangelical efforts amply bears witness.

This, then, is a thumbnail historical sketch of Mormonism yesterday and today. Now let us consider the doctrines which Mormons hold and teach as necessary for

membership in the "true" church of Jesus Christ, the Latter-day Saints.

STATEMENT OF FAITH

The statement of faith published by the Mormon church reads in many places like a declaration of orthodox theology; however, it is in reality a clever and, I believe, deliberate attempt to deceive the naive into believing that Mormonism is a Christian religion, which it is not in any sense of the term. All Mormons recognize Joseph Smith as a prophet and his words as binding, and thus the words of Smith carry as much if not more authority than the revealed Word of God. Mormonism differs from evangelical Christianity in five major ways and in numerous minor points which time does not allow us to discuss here.

1) Mormons deny the Scriptural doctrine of the Trinity and the deity of the Lord Jesus Christ. To the Mormon mind God is a corporeal being even as we are, literally flesh and bones, and in the words of Bringham Young: "Adam is our father and our God and the only God with whom we have to do."[8] Historically, Mormon theology teaches that Adam-God entered Eden with Eve, one of His celestial wives, and the result of this physical union produced the human race. Further than this, Joseph Smith himself wrote: "The Father has a body of flesh and bones . . . the Son also; but the Holy Ghost has not a body of flesh and bones but is

---

[8] Brigham Young, *Journal of Discourses*, 1:50. Some Mormon apologists state that Brigham Young mentioned these things and may have taught them, but deny it was so interpreted by the Church. However, this is refuted completely by the statement of President Wilfred Woodruff, who confirmed it as Young's doctrine (*Journal of Wilfred Woodruff*, April 10, 1825), as well as by Brigham Young's proclamation that God revealed the Adam-God doctrine to him (*Deseret News*, June 18, 1873). Recently the Mormon Church rejected officially the Adam-God doctrine of Young and his contemporaries but declined to admit that Young ever taught it. This is a classic case of trying to have one's cake and eat it too.

a personage of Spirit."[9] It may be seen from this that the Mormon concept of God is completely foreign to that given in the Bible, for as Christ Himself said, "God is Spirit, and they that worship him must worship him in spirit and in truth" (John 4:24). Mormonism seeks to reduce God to a carnal plane and even ascribes to Him human methods of reproduction fully in keeping with the immoral and polygamous characters of Smith and Young, who allegedly had 41 and 26 wives respectively, and the latter 56 children.

2) Mormonism denies the authority of the Bible and, as has been shown, flatly contradicts the very Savior in whom they profess to believe. The Bible clearly teaches that it, as interpreted by the Holy Spirit, is the sole authority for faith and morals, but Mormons equate *The Book of Mormon* with the Bible despite the fact that it has been shown to be a gigantic fraud and very possibly a deliberate plagiarism on the part of Smith and his cohort.

3) Historic Mormon theology denies the virgin birth of our Lord Jesus Christ and maintains instead that He was not conceived by the Holy Spirit but by Adam-God, who descended to earth and generated Jesus in the womb of Mary by sexual union. This shocking and vile concept is found in the writings of Brigham Young, who shamelessly wrote: "When the virgin Mary conceived the child Jesus the Father had begotten Him in His own likeness. He was not begotten by the Holy Ghost. And who was the Father? He was the first of the human family [Adam]."[10] One could search all the pages of Greek mythology and never surpass this display of sensual wickedness, and yet almost 3 ½ million people apply such blasphemy to the Son of God, who, Scripture tells us, was generated by the Holy Spirit and born of the virgin Mary without the aid of human agency (Luke 1:3-35).

---

[9] Joseph Smith, *Doctrine and Covenants*, p. 462.
[10] B. Young, *loc cit.* See also Brigham Young, *Discourses of Brigham Young*, p. 50.

4) The Mormon Church denies emphatically the great and true Biblical doctrine of justification before God on the basis of faith alone. The Apostle Paul tells us, "Therefore, being justified by faith, we have peace with God through our Lord Jesus Christ" (Romans 5:1). Indeed, the foundation stone of our hope is that God has nothing against us, has forgiven our sins because Christ has died in our place. But a far different view is espoused by the Mormon Church, as witnessed by their teaching: "The sectarian dogma of justification by faith alone has exercised an influence for evil since the early days of Christianity."[11] It is a fairly simple matter to see from this bold declaration that Mormonism holds no brief for the Bible; indeed, it is apparent that the Bible is only a convenient tool by which they attract attention to their subtle and ever-misleading dogmas of deception.

5) The Mormon doctrine of the atonement of Christ is a far different one from that revealed in the Bible. The Scriptures irrevocably teach that Christ the "Lamb of God" (John 1:29) "bare in his own body our sins on the tree" (1 Peter 2:24), and that His blood alone is efficacious for the penalty of human sin. We are constantly reminded in the Bible that Christ died to purchase for us eternal life; not a sensual earthly paradise thriving on polygamy and the indulgence of human lusts, but a home "eternal in the heavens," one that "fadeth not away." This is a far cry from Mormon mythology, which, like Russellism, teaches that all the atonement purchased for man was a "resurrection," an earthly paradise with the prospect of everlasting fertility and connubial bliss in the tradition of King Solomon's harem! In the words of the late President John Taylor of the Mormon Church: ". . . what was lost in Adam was restored in Christ. . . . Transgressions of the law brought death upon all the posterity of Adam, the restoration through the atonement restored all the human

---

[11] James E. Talmadge, *The Articles of Faith*, p. 480.

family to life. . . . The atonement made by Jesus Christ resulted in the resurrection of the human body."[12] It would be possible to enumerate many, many more differences between orthodox Christianity and the theology of Mormonism, but these are all discussed in my books *The Maze of Mormonism* and *The Kingdom of the Cults.*

The menace of Mormonism is the fact that it cleverly coats large doses of error with a thin layer of sugary half-truths and seemingly plausible reasons. By setting up a scale of punishment and sensuous rewards after death, Mormonism appeals to many persons who do not feel they are bad enough to go to hell nor good enough to go straight to heaven, but who like the idea of a place where suffering does not exist but exile and a chance for future glory does. This proves most attractive to numerous individuals who do not have a sound grounding in Biblical theology. To board the Mormon train one needs a strong imagination, a supreme ego, and a firm conviction that no church on earth is true except the one founded by the "Prophet" Joseph Smith. The ego is needed because Mormon males believe they are potentially gods (in a higher or lower sense depending upon their faithfulness to the "Prophet" and his teachings) and that their destiny is sealed. They believe that someday they shall rule a polygamous universe presided over by their flesh-and-bone god, innumerable celestial wives, and "Prophet" Smith.[13]

In the light of these startling facts and the alarming spread and popularity of the Mormon religion, devout Christians must now take a definite stand; we can hesitate no longer. Four steps are needed immediately, I believe, to check the Mormon menace. They are as follows:

1. A program of education aimed at aiding pastors, teachers, and laymen to recognize the threat of Mormonism and the need for strong countermeasures.

---

[12] John Taylor, *The Mediation and Atonement*, pp. 170, 177, 178.
[13] To put it plainly in the words of Lorenzo Snow, former Mormon leader: "As man is, God once was—As God is, man may become.

2. The circulation of up-to-date and factual literature on the history, doctrines, and methods of Mormon progress, especially in the Midwest, on the Pacific Coast, and in Hawaii.

3. A continual supply to worldwide mission fields of information on Mormon missionary activities, so that Mormonism may be kept under constant surveillance both at home and abroad.

4. A steady flow of consecrated Christian doctrine through churches, Bible schools, colleges, and seminaries dedicated to training our future leaders in a sound apologetic background so vital to combatting all forms of false doctrine which appear so prevalent in these the last days of the age of grace.

It is the fundamental thesis of this writer that until Christians everywhere realize the danger of the cultism so clearly portrayed in the rise of the Mormon cult, evangelical efforts will continue to suffer on all mission fields, foreign and domestic, from those people of whom our Lord warned us, "Beware of false prophets, which come to you in sheep's clothing, but inwardly they are ravening wolves" (Matthew 7:15).

Let us awake to the dangers before us: the cultist wolf is at the door of the sheepfold. "He that hath ears to hear, let him hear."

Five

THE CRUX OF CHRISTIAN SCIENCE

The religion of Christian Science has since its earliest beginnings presented a challenge to orthodox Christianity by widely advertising its power to heal sickness. Within the ranks of the Christian Science Church today are to be found many thousands of former churchgoing folk who held membership in our major denominations.[1] These persons are Christian Scientists today mainly because at one time in their lives they underwent some type of "healing" which they attributed to the "revelation" given by Mary Baker Eddy, as found in her textbook *Science and Health, With Key to the Scriptures.*

Christian Science has offered to these people a sanctuary from the preaching of the gospel of Christ, which points out the terrible reality of sin and evil in man's nature and strips from the soul every vestige of self-righteousness. Mrs. Eddy's religion, on the other hand, offers no such hazards, denying as it does the existence of evil, sin, sickness, and even death itself.

The average Christian Scientist can well afford, therefore, to remain oblivious to the necessity of repentance from sin and faith in the blood of the Lamb, which Mrs. Eddy discounts entirely in its vicarious Biblical application.[2]

---

[1] Current church membership is reputed to be in excess of a half-million persons.

[2] *Science and Health, With Key to the Scriptures*, p. 330. (References are always to 1895 edition unless otherwise noted.)

The theology of Christian Science prohibits any acceptance whatsoever of the vicarious atonement of our Lord, and blatantly denies eternal retribution for those who willfully reject Jesus Christ as "the Lamb of God, who taketh away the sin of the world" (John 1:29).[3]

Throughout this chapter on Christian Science, then, I shall ask you to keep in mind these things, and to remember that Mrs. Eddy's textbook and various writings are considered virtually infallible by all true Christian Scientists, who own her, living or dead, as their "beloved Leader."

With these thoughts in mind, let us now consider the history, theology, and peculiarities of Christian Science, one of the fastest-growing cults in America, and one of the most dedicated enemies of the evangelical Christian faith.

Mary Ann Morse Baker, the future Mrs. Eddy, was born in Bow, New Hampshire, in the year 1821 to Mark and Abigail Baker, hearty farmers and staunch Congregationalists by religion. During her childhood Mary Baker was quite sickly and given to fits of depression and extreme temper, which made life with her at that period almost intolerable.[4]

In the year 1843, at the age of 22, Mary Baker married George W. Glover, the first of her three husbands and most probably her one great love. The first marriage of Mary Baker ended almost as soon as it began, for less than seven months later George W. Glover was stricken with yellow fever while on a trip to Wilmington, North Carolina.[5] The death of her husband prostrated the young wife, who was then about to bear her first and only child, George W. Glover, Jr. Later in life Mrs. Eddy adopted another son, Dr.

---

[3] Ibid., p. 579.

[4] E. F. Dakin, *Mrs. Eddy* (New York: Charles Scribner's Sons, 1929), pp. 6, 7, 19.

[5] The Glovers had been living in Charleston, S.C., since their marriage.

E. J. Foster Eddy, who at one time took charge of publishing her book *Science and Health.*

After the death of George Glover, Sr., the widowed Mary Glover returned to her father's home in Tilton, New Hampshire, where her child was born and subsequently reared.

The second marriage of Mary Baker Glover was contracted almost ten years to the day after her first husband had died, and was to Dr. Daniel Patterson, a handsome and amorous dentist whom she later divorced, charging adultery, though such was never conclusively proved.

The final marriage of Mary Baker Glover Patterson was to one Asa G. Eddy, a student of Christian Science, whose meek temperament led him to acquiesce to her every whim with perfect obedience. The last marriage of Mrs. Eddy strangely enough caused her more trouble publicly than either of the previous two, for upon the death of Asa, Mrs. Eddy claimed that he had been killed by arsenic poison.[6]

This rather strange diagnosis aroused the medical profession considerably, and she was denounced for even entertaining such a diagnosis. Mrs. Eddy's chief witness for her diagnostic efforts was "Dr." C.J. Eastman, Dean of the Bellevue Medical College, who was later exposed as a quack abortioner and sentenced to prison, and his college closed. "Dr." Eastman's opinions were therefore utterly worthless, and, as the autopsy on Asa disclosed, he died of a chronic heart condition, just as Dr. Rufus Noyes, the attending physician, had originally declared.[7]

MRS. EDDY VERSUS DR. QUIMBY AND THE TRUTH

The name Phineas Quimby has always been a sore spot in the thriving body that is Mrs. Eddy's religion, for it is a

---

[6] See *The Boston Post*, June 5, 1882.

[7] See my booklet *Christian Science* (Minneapolis: Bethany Fellowship, 1976).

fact accepted by all impartial students of the Eddy religion, excepting Christian Scientists and their sympathizers, that Mrs. Eddy was indebted to this man for the basic principles upon which she built her faith.

Phineas Parkhurst Quimby was from his early adulthood interested in mental phenomena of one kind or another. "Dr." Quimby was for some years a professional mesmerist before he became interested in the possibilities of utilizing hypnosis and suggestion for the curing of certain organic manifestations of diseases. Dr. Quimby also used the terms "the science of the Christ" and "Christian Science" (1863) years before Mrs. Eddy ever adopted them.[8]

It was as the result of a spinal affliction that Mrs. Eddy came to Maine to visit Dr. Quimby, who was then practicing in Portland.[9] Born in 1802 in Belfast, Quimby was almost sixty years old and at the height of his success as a mental healer when Mrs. Eddy visited him.

The effect that the old Maine healer had on Mrs. Eddy was truly astonishing, for in the November 7th edition of *The Portland Evening Courier* she lauded him for miraculously curing her and declared that she was "improving ad infinitum."[10] Upon the death of Dr. Quimby in January of 1866, Mrs. Eddy was deeply affected and wrote a stirring poem praising Quimby's memory and abilities. In later years, however, when Mrs. Eddy was charged with pirating Quimby's ideas to form the basis of her book *Science and Health* (1875), she spoke of Quimby in anything but complimentary terms, referring to him as "illiterate" and "a very unlearned man," etc., though she admitted privately to her literary adviser, the Reverend J. H. Wiggin, that the charges were essentially true.[11]

---

[8] Horatio Dresses, *The Quimby Manuscripts*, p. 388.

[9] October, 1862.

[10] Mrs. Eddy also claimed that Quimby healed as Christ did, as in her own words, "P. P. Quimby . . . heals as never man healed since Christ." See Georgine Milmine, *The Life of Mary Baker Eddy*, p. 60.

[11] See Livingstone Wright, *How Rev. Wiggin Rewrote Mrs. Eddy's Book*, p. 41.

That Mrs. Eddy had access to Quimby's ideas and even owned a copy of one of his manuscripts (*Questions and Answers*), which contains changes in her own handwriting, no competent scholar denies. For a comparison of this manuscript with Mrs. Eddy's writings, see *The New York Times*, July 10, 1904.

The attempt, therefore, to discredit Quimby's influence upon Mrs. Eddy and her textbook has never been relaxed by the Christian Scientists and their supporters, proof of which is found in Sibyl Wilbur's biography of Mrs. Eddy,[12] the official publication of the Church, and Norman Beasley's *The Cross and the Crown*, wherein Quimby is dismissed, all evidence to the contrary. The facts, however, still remain, and any fair-minded person will have little difficulty in ascertaining that Mrs. Eddy is not "the discoverer and founder of a new religion" at all, but merely the instrument which expanded and recognized the teachings of P. P. Quimby, the father of Christian Science.

It would be possible to go on at great length and thoroughly document the Quimby-Eddy controversy, but this has all been covered in detail,[13] so we shall pass over any further discussion of this facet of the Eddy religion and continue with our evaluation of its leader.

During the course of her long, eventful life (89 years), Mary Baker Eddy displayed a phenomenal ability for making money. In fact, she once said to the Reverend J. H. Wiggin, her literary editor: "Mr. Wiggin, Christian Science is a good thing. I make ten thousand a year at it."[14]

For Mrs. Eddy it certainly proved to be just that. At her death she had amassed several million dollars, of which not one cent was given to charity.

"Mother" Eddy, as she was known to the faithful, invented many ways to garner the lonely dollars in the pockets of her followers, from virtually ordering her sub-

---

[12] Sibyl Wilbur, *The Life of Mary Baker Eddy*, pp. 93-101.
[13] See Georgina Milmine's work previously cited.
[14] Wright, *op. cit.*, pp. 45, 46.

jects to buy and sell her books, under penalty of excommunication from her church,[15] to "requesting" contributions for "three tea jackets" for "Mother" to wear.[16]

At one time in her career as promoter, Mrs. Eddy even endorsed the purchase of silver and gold spoons upon which a scrap of her sacred writings was inscribed in bas relief.[17] It is no wonder, then, that for her at least, Christian Science was a very "good thing."

As to the often-trumpeted "power to heal" that Christian Scientists claim for Mrs. Eddy, little need be said here, but it is deserving of at least one condensed statement to show that it too is part of the Eddy legend.

In *The New York Sun* of December 19, 1898, Mrs. Eddy boldly "challenged the world to disprove" that she had healed "consumption in the last stages . . . malignant tubercular diphtheria. . . . carious bones. . . . a cancer that had so eaten the flesh of the neck as to expose the jugular vein. . . ." This challenge was quickly accepted by Dr. Charles A. L. Reed of Cincinnati, later President of the American Medical Association, in *The Sun* of January 1, 1899, in which he offered to present Mrs. Eddy with similar cases and "if she, by her Christian Science, shall cure any one of them, I shall proclaim her omnipotence from the housetops; and, if she shall cure all, or even half of them, I shall cheerfully crawl upon my hands and knees that I may but touch the hem of her walking-dress." Dr. Reed even offered to make arrangements for Mrs. Eddy to "heal at one visit" identical cases then under treatment at Bellevue or "some other New York Hospital" to spare her the fatigue of a trip to Cincinnati. The eminent physician completed his offer in the following words, which are noted for their fair analysis of the issue then at hand:

> If Mrs. Eddy will accept this challenge and cure one or more of the cases, she will thereby demonstrate that

---

15 *The Christian Science Journal*, March 1897.
16 *Ibid.*, December 21, 1899.
17 *Ibid.*, February 18, 1909.

she may be something more than either a conscienceless speculator on human credulity or an unfortunate victim of egotistic alienation.

Mrs. Eddy never accepted Dr. Reed's offer, nor did she care to discuss the matter at length again, and for a very good reason later revealed during the cross-examination of Mr. Alfred Farlow[18] by F. W. Peabody, noted Boston lawyer and implacable enemy of Christian Science. Mr. Farlow was at the time Chairman of the Publication Committee of the Christian Science Church and President of the Mother Church in Boston, and was therefore in an excellent position to know the facts about Mrs. Eddy. Yet he swore under oath that he did not know of *any* healing ever having been made by Mrs. Eddy of *any* organic disease in her entire life, except *stiff leg!*

These facts, then, show quite plainly that Mrs. Eddy's claim to divine healing power was indeed evidence of a most vital truth deadly to the cause of Christian Science—the truth that Mrs. Eddy never healed as she claimed, could not heal properly diagnosed organic diseases when challenged, and dared not put her vaunted powers to an open test. Let those who enter Christian Science take with them this warning in the light of these facts: Mary Baker Eddy did not heal, as her zealous disciples maintain; in fact, she made use of medical care herself in later years, both doctors and dentists, and even utilized morphine as a pain-killer for her various "attacks."[19]

As we have briefly examined Christian Science, we have found that its originator was not Mrs. Eddy, but Dr. Quimby. We have seen that Mrs. Eddy utilized Quimby's material openly, while alternately praising and damning the old gentleman. And we have shown her claims to divine inspiration and healing to be a myth erected painstakingly by her zealous lackeys. To be sure, there is some good in the

---

18 F. W. Peabody, *The Religio-Medical Masquerade*, p. 113.
19 See *The New York World*, May 8, 1907, and E. F. Dakin, *Mrs. Eddy*, pp. 513, 514.

Christian Science religion, but whatever goodness there is, is a borrowed goodness, and it remains a fact that the Christian Science religion plays fast and loose with both the Bible and its terminology to the glory of Mrs. Eddy.

Relative to the many alleged "cures" in Christian Science, much has already been written; hence only a cursory notice needs to be made here.

There is very little doubt in the mind of the author that a great many "cures" recorded by the Christian Science Church are psychosomatic in nature, induced by suggestion and a concentrated form of psychotherapy which at times has the appearance of a miraculous intervention. As Dr. David Davis of Bellevue has said, "What has been induced by suggestion can be removed by suggestion," and this is doubtless true of some of the accomplishments of Mrs. Eddy's practitioners.

Similarly, there are seemingly verifiable cases of healings by Christian Scientists, of both fellow Scientists and non-Scientists, which apparently defy contradiction and are, I believe, a direct fulfillment of what Christ warned us of in His famous discourse as recorded in Matthew 7:15-23. Contrary to popular opinion, healing is not always a sign of divine favor, and never so when it is effected by those who deny the authority of the Scriptures and the very Christ in whose name they claim to heal.[20] Christian Scientists deny both the authority of Scripture[21] and the deity of Christ,[22] and therefore it is of them, among others, that Jesus warned His disciples and us. Let us therefore be diligent lest we be deceived by those whose powers are after the workings of Satan, "with signs and lying wonders."

---

[20] The Bible clearly teaches that Satan's emissaries can also duplicate miracles, as in the case of Moses and the Egyptian magicians as recorded in the Book of Exodus (7:11, 22; 8:7, 18). Wonders do not always mean that God is working, for He works only to the glory of Jesus Christ and in perfect accord with Christian doctrine.

[21] *Miscellaneous Writings*, pp. 169, 170.

[22] *Ibid*, p. 84.

In completing this outline of Christian Science it is my conviction that a series of quotations from Christian Science sources will prove helpful to the average reader who has neither the time nor possibly the inclination to hunt up all the pertinent facts relative to the peculiar doctrines of Mrs. Eddy's religion.

To enable such readers to have this valuable source material at their fingertips, I have listed sixteen of the major doctrines of Christianity, together with contradictory quotations taken directly from Mrs. Eddy's writings. These comparisons will, we believe, provide sufficient documentation should a dispute ever arise concerning the classification of Christian Science as a Christian religion.[23]

Inspiration of the Bible

1. Referring to Genesis 2:7: "Is this addition to His creation real or unreal? Is it the truth? Or is it a lie, concerning man and God? It must be the latter . . . " (*Science and Health*, p. 517).

2. " . . . the manifest mistakes in the ancient versions; the thirty thousand different readings in the Old Testament, and the three hundred thousand in the New,—these facts show how a mortal and material sense stole into the divine record, darkening, to some extent, the inspired pages with its own hue" (*Science and Health*, p. 33).

The Doctrine of the Trinity and the Deity of Christ

1. "The theory of three persons in one God (that is, a personal Trinity or Tri-unity) suggests heathen gods, rather than the one ever-present I AM" (*Science and Health*, p. 152).

2. "The Christian who believes in the First Commandment is a monotheist. Thus he virtually unites with the Jews' belief in one God and recognizes that Jesus Christ *is not* God as Jesus Himself declared, but is the Son of God" (*Science and Health* [1914], p. 361).

---

[23] All quotations from the book *Miscellaneous Writings* are from the edition of 1897, and all quotations from *Science and Health* are from the edition of 1895 unless specifically designated otherwise.

3. "The spiritual Christ was infallible; Jesus, as material manhood, *was not* Christ" (*Miscellaneous Writings*, p. 84).

The Doctrine of God and the Holy Spirit

1. "In that name of Jehovah the true idea of God seems almost lost. He becomes 'a man of war,' a tribal god to be worshipped,—rather than Love, the divine Principle to be lived and loved" (*Science and Health*, p. 517).
2. "GOD: Principle, Life, Truth, Love, Soul, Spirit, Mind" (*Science and Health*, p. 9).
3. "God is all . . . the soul, or mind, of the spiritual man is God, the divine Principle of all being" (*Science and Health* [1914], p. 302).

The Virgin Birth of Christ

1. "A portion of God could not enter corporeal mortal man; neither could His feelings be reflected by Him, or God would be manifestly finite, lose the deific character, and become less than God" (*Science and Health*, p. 231).
2. "Jesus, the Galilean prophet, was born of the virgin Mary's spiritual thoughts of life and its manifestation" (*The First Church of Christ, Scientist and Miscellany*, p. 261).

The Doctrine of Miracles

1. "The sick are not healed merely by declaring there is no sickness, but by knowing that there is none" (*Science and Health* [1914], p. 447).
2. "A mere request that God will heal the sick has no power to gain more of the divine presence than is always at hand" (*Science and Health*, p. 317).
3. "The so-called miracles contained in Holy Writ are neither supernatural or preternatural . . . Jesus regarded good as the normal state of mind and evil as the abnormal. . . . The so-called pains and pleasures of matter were alike unreal to Jesus; for He regarded matter as only a vagary of mortal belief, and subdued it with this understanding" (*Miscellaneous Writings*, pp. 200, 201).

The Atonement of Jesus Christ

1. "The material blood of Jesus was no more efficacious to cleanse from sin when it was shed upon 'the accursed tree' than when it was flowing in His veins, as He went daily about His Father's business" (*Science and Health*, p. 330)

2. "The real atonement—so infinitely beyond the heathen conception that God requires human blood to propitiate His justice and bring His mercy—needs to be understood. . . . He (Jesus) suffered, to show mortals the awful price paid by sin and how to avoid paying it. He atoned for the terrible unreality of a supposed existence apart from God. He suffered because of the shocking human idolatry that presupposes Life, Substance, Soul and Intelligence in matter . . ." (*No and Yes* [1893], pp. 44, 45).

The Death and Resurrection of Christ

1. "Jesus' students, not sufficiently advanced to fully understand their Master's triumph, did not perform many wonderful works until they saw Him after His crucifixion and learned that *He had not died*" (*Science and Health*, pp. 350, 351).

2. "His disciples believed Jesus dead while He was hiding in the sepulchre, whereas He was alive, demonstrating, within the narrow tomb, the power of the Spirit to destroy human, material sense" (*Science and Health*, p. 349).

The Ascension and Second Coming of Christ

1. "Through all the disciples beheld, they became more spiritual and understood better what the Master had taught. . . . They needed this quickening, for soon their dear Master would rise again in the spiritual scale of existence, and fly far beyond their apprehension. As the reward for His faithfulness He would disappear to material sense, in that change which has since been called the Ascension" (*Science and Health*, p. 339).

Satan and the Existence of Evil

1. "The beliefs of the human mind rob and enslave it, and then impute this result to another elusive personification, named Satan" (*Science and Health*, p. 81).

2. "There was never a moment in which evil was real" (*No and Yes*, p. 33).

The Nature and Existence of Hell

1. "The sinner makes his own hell by doing evil, and saint his own heaven by doing right" (*Science and Health* [1914], p. 266).
2. "The olden opinion that hell is fire and brimstone has yielded somewhat to the metaphysical fact that suffering is a thing of mortal mind instead of body; so, in place of material flames and odor, mental anguish is generally accepted as the penalty for sin" (*Miscellaneous Writings*, p. 237).

The Kingdom of Heaven—Its Reality and Significance

1. Definition: "Heaven, Harmony: the reign of Spirit; government by Principle; spirituality; bliss; the atmosphere of Soul" (*Science and Health*, p. 578).
2. "Heaven is harmony,—infinite bliss—Heaven is the reign of Divine Science" (*First Church of Christ, Scientist and Miscellany*, p. 267).

The Doctrine of Eternal Salvation

1. "Man as God's idea is already saved with an everlasting salvation" (*Miscellaneous Writings*, p. 261).
2. "Final deliverance from error—whereby we rejoice in immortality, boundless freedom, and sinless sense—is neither reached through paths of flowers, nor by pinning one's faith to another's vicarious effort" (*Science and Health*, p. 327).

The Doctrine of Prayer

1. "Prayer can neither change God, nor bring his designs into mortal modes—I have no objection to audible prayer of the right kind; but inaudible is more effectual" (*No and Yes*, pp. 48, 50).
2. "If prayer nourishes the belief that sin is cancelled, and that man is made better by merely praying, it is an evil. He grows worse, who continues in sin because he thinks himself forgiven" (*Science and Health*, p. 311).

The Creation of Matter and Its Reality

1. "There is . . . no intelligent sin, evil mind or matter; and this is the only true philosophy and realism" (*No and Yes*, p. 47).
2. "There is no Life, Truth, intelligence or substance in matter, but all is infinite Mind and its infinite manifestation, for God is All in all" (*Science and Health* [1914], p. 468).

Man, the Soul, His True Nature and Destiny

1. "Man originated not from dust, materially, but from Spirit, spiritually" (*Miscellaneous Writings*, p. 57).
2. "Man is God's image and likeness; whatever is possible to God, is possible to man as God's reflection" (*Miscellaneous Writings*, p. 183).

The Existence of Sin, Sickness, and Death

1. "Being destroyed, sin needs no other form of forgiveness. . . . Since God is All, there is no room for His opposite . . . therefore evil, being the opposite of goodness, is unreal . . . for the sinner is making a reality of sin—making that real which is unreal. . . . Only those who repent of sin, and forsake all evil, can fully understand the unreality of evil. . . . To get rid of sin, through Science, is to divest sin of any supposed mind or reality, and never to admit that sin can have intelligence or power, pain or pleasure. You can conquer error by denying its verity" (*Science and Health*, p. 234).
2. "Death. An illusion, for there is no death; the unreal and untrue; the opposite of Good, God, or Life. . . . Any material evidence of death is false, for it contradicts the spiritual facts of Being" (*Science and Health*, p. 575).
3. "To put down the claim of sin you must detect it, remove the mask, point out the illusion, and thus get the victory over sin, and prove its unreality" (*Science and Health*, p. 444).

Biblical Texts Helpful in Refuting Christian Science Theology

1. *The Authority of the Bible*: Psalm 119:140; Isaiah 40:8; Matthew 24:35; John 10:35; 17:17; 2 Timothy 3:16.

2. *The Trinity and the Death of Christ:* Genesis 1:26; 11:7; 18:1-33; Exodus 3:14; Isaiah 6:8; 9:6; John 1:1, 14; 8:58; Colossians 1:15; 2:9; Hebrews 1:3; Revelation 1:7, 8, 16.

3. *The Personality of the Holy Spirit:* Luke 12:12; John 16:7, 8; Acts 13:2; 5:1-5.

4. *The Virgin Birth and Miracles of Jesus:* Isaiah 7:14; 9:6; Micah 5:2; Matthew 1:18-25; 8:14, 15, 26, 27; 9:2, 6, 7, 27-30; Luke 1:30-38. Miracles: Mark 1:32-34; John 2:1-11; 6:10-14.

5. *The Atonement, Death, and Resurrection of Christ:* Exodus 12:13; Leviticus 17:11; Psalm 22; Isaiah 53; Daniel 9:26; Matthew 26:28; 28:5-7; Luke 24:39; John 1:29; 19:33; Romans 5:6-8; Ephesians 1:7; Colossians 1:20.

6. *The Doctrine of Eternal Retribution:* Matthew 13:42, 50; 22:13; Mark 9:44, 46, 48; Luke 3:17; Revelation 20:10.

7. *The Doctrine of Christian Prayer:* Matthew 6:5-15; 7:7-11; Luke 18:1; Philippians 4:6; 1 Thessalonians 5:17;

8. *The Doctrine of Sin:* Romans 3:23; 6:23; 1 John 1:10; 3:4; 5:17.

Six

THE UNITY SCHOOL OF CHRISTIANITY

There are many types and shades of heresy to be found today within the borders of Christendom which deserve the concerned attention of all true Christians everywhere. Principal among these non-Christian cults is The Unity School of Christianity, or Unity, as the faithful often term it. This up-and-growing concern first entered the arena of non-Christian cults in the year 1889, when Myrtle and Charles Fillmore first promulgated their "new" revelation. From this union of wills, a humble origin to be sure, Unity has grown to astronomical proportions. Unity is also very propaganda-conscious in that it concentrates very heavily on the power of the printed page. Yearly it speaks in millions of tracts, pamphlets, magazines, and books to advertise America's biggest mail-order religion.

Openly rivaling the propaganda activities of Jehovah's Witnesses, Christian Science, and Mormonism, Unity continues to grow in power and prestige throughout America, especially in the Midwest. The activities of Unity are not restricted to "Air Mail" or "Special Delivery" salvation; however, over its own and numerous other radio stations the movement broadcasts its "soothing" remedies for everything from sin, sickness, and death to domestic troubles and the incessant demands of finance companies. Unity teaches that there is no problem insoluble if one "practices" its tenets faithfully, and offers not only health and happiness but financial security as well. Couple, if you will, these material benefits with an extremely palatable theology—palatable, that is, to those uninstructed in the Word of God—and one can easily see why Unity is a "sure-fire" prospect for popularity and expansion.

Today, the Unity School of Christianity boasts over 2.5 million members, many well-edited magazines, a huge printing operation in Lee Summit, Missouri (its head-quarters), a Sunday-school quarterly (*Wee Wisdom*), and a restaurant for vegetarians that has no equal for either variety or quality.

Charles Fillmore supervised the entire facilities of his huge empire until death claimed him in 1948, a well-advanced octogenarian. Myrtle Fillmore, his wife, partner, and cofounder of Unity, "passed on" in 1931. However, the aging prophet of eternal youth subsequently married Cora Dedrick, his secretary, who survived him, along with a son by his first marriage.

The literature of Unity Christianity is published in the best taste; the paper is good and the bindings are excellent. The style of writing is also very appealing, since it makes much use of Biblical references and illustrations. Unfortunately, the average person who either listens to a Unity broadcast or reads from its numerous publications doubtless believes Unity to be a form of Christian theology. But it is not, in any sane use of the word, as I shall now demonstrate conclusively from its own written propaganda.

Like other non-Christian cults, the Unity School of Christianity adopts Biblical language to ensnare the unwary layman. But the elusive specter of deceit, so prevalent in Unity and obvious to the trained eye, must be projected starkly against the backdrop of Biblical revelation and stripped of its protective mimicry. Once this has been accomplished, the entire system is revealed as a gigantic masquerade and fraud, a clever counterfeit of the true gospel.

UNITY VERSUS THE TRIUNE GOD

"The Father is Principle, the Son is that Principle revealed in a creative plan, the Holy Spirit is the executive power of both Father and Son carrying out the creative plan."[1]

The Unity School commits one of the basic errors of Christian Science in that it makes God the same as Love, and in the next breath reverses the proposition, making Love the same as God. One can easily see from this that God thereby becomes impersonal, which concept is the direct antithesis of all Biblical revelations concerning the Person and nature of God. "God is loving. . . . God does not love anybody. . . . God is the love in everybody and everything. . . . God is love. . . . God exercises none of his attributes except through the inner consciousness of the universe and man."[2]

From the preceding quotation, we feel that it is quite evident that Unity in no sense worships the personal God of the Bible, the God and Father of our Lord Jesus Christ. It would be possible to list many more perversions of the Biblical concept of God from Unity literature, but none speaks more clearly against the doctrine of the triune God than does the abject pantheism of the definition found in Unity's *Metaphysical Dictionary*. One cannot have been born into God's family by the Holy Spirit nor washed in the blood of the Lamb unless he feels the utmost revulsion in the depths of his soul for Unity's complete unconcern for truth as revealed in the foregoing quotations. The Father objectively loved the world, hence He is a Person who is capable of love, not love itself, as Unity would have us believe.

For Unity, then, the God of the Bible is an impersonal "It," a Principle, Supreme Intelligence, Divine Mind, etc. In no sense, they teach, is He a personal Being.

It must be very evident to even the most adamant Unity adherent that the voice of the Lord speaks most clearly through the Scriptures, bearing testimony to His personal Being, as distinguished from Unity's pantheistic, un-

---

[1] *Metaphysical Bible Dictionary* (Unity School of Christianity), p. 629.

[2] *Jesus Christ Heals*, (Unity School of Christianity, 1944), pp. 31, 32.

Christian concept of God. The attempts of the Unity School to obscure this great Biblical doctrine with a confusion of terminology pales beside the triumphant witness of the Law, the Prophets, and the Christ, that God is personal, as He has countless times proclaimed in His Word: "Look unto me, and be ye saved, all the ends of the earth: for I am God, and there is none else" (Isaiah 45:22). Biblically speaking, then, Unity fails in its basic premise—a non-Christian definition of God which at one time describes Him as neuter, and at another time makes Him both masculine and feminine—errors shared, incidentally, by Christian Science.[3]

UNITY VERSUS THE BIBLE

Throughout the whole content of Unity's vast storehouse of printed propaganda, literally thousands of times the Bible is perverted and misinterpreted at direct variance with its own language and context by numerous Unity propagandists who are admittedly ignorant of the basic languages of the Bible and therefore totally unqualified to engage in deep exegetical translations of the original texts. No better illustration can be given of this than the almost-sickening "metaphysical interpretation" of Psalm 23, as recorded in the late Charles Fillmore's book *Prosperity*.[4]

> The Lord is my banker; my credit is good. He maketh me to lie down in the consciousness of omnipotent abundance. He giveth me the key to His strongbox. He restoreth my faith in His riches. He guideth me in the paths of prosperity for His name's sake. Yes, though I walk through the very shadow of debt, I shall fear no evil, for Thou art with me; Thy silver and gold, they secure me. Thou preparest a way for me in the presence of the collector; Thou fillest my wallet with plenty; my measure runneth over. Surely, goodness and plenty will follow me all the days of my life; and I shall do business in the name of the Lord forever.

---

[3] Unity Statement of Faith, Articles 16 and 32.
[4] P. 60.

Any reasonably intelligent individual cannot fail to see that this interpretation by Fillmore is a direct and absolute perversion of David's Psalm, which stressed dependence upon a personal God, not a glorified impersonal banker. Space does not permit a detailed analysis of this cult's further assaults upon God's Word. However, the interested reader may obtain a thorough study which is both historical and theological, including a full and detailed refutation of the Unity movement, in my book *Kingdom of the Cults*.[5]

UNITY VERSUS THE DEITY, PERSON, AND WORK OF CHRIST

"We do most certainly accept the Divinity of Christ and of Jesus Christ, and we believe most thoroughly in the work which he did for mankind."[6] The average Christian (or non-Christian layman for that matter) who peruses the literature of Unity would doubtless accept the above statement at face value. Yet, like the ancient Gnostics, Unity denies the complete and absolute deity of Jesus of Nazareth and insists instead that He and "the Christ, "the Spiritual Identity of Jesus," are two separate entities.

The Bible says that God so loved the world that he gave his only begotten Son, but the Bible does not here refer to Jesus of Nazareth, the outer man; it refers to the Christ, the spiritual identity of Jesus, whom he acknowledged in all his ways, and brought forth into his outer, until even the flesh of his body was lifted up, purified, spiritualized, and redeemed. Thus he became Jesus Christ, the Word made flesh. And we are to follow into this perfect state and become like him, for in each of us is the Christ, the only begotten Son. We can, through Jesus Christ, our Redeemer and Example, bring forth the Christ within us, the true self of all men, and be made perfect even as our

---

[5] See especially Chapter 14.
[6] *Unity*, Vol. 72, No. 2, p. 8.

Father in heaven is perfect, as Jesus Christ commanded his followers to be.[7]

The Bible declares that the Eternal Word of God (John 1:1) became Man in Jesus of Nazareth (John 1:14) and that He never ceased to be the Deity—that He was and ever shall be (Philippians 2:8; Colossians 2:9; John 8:58; Revelation 1:7, 18; etc.). Jesus Christ was not Jesus *and* Christ, as the Gnostics and Unity cultists would have us believe; rather, He was the God-Man, two natures in one Being, immutable forever.

The interested reader should know the following quoted examples of repeated term-switching, all applied by them to man, but Biblically applied only to Jesus Christ. "I am the Son of God" (Matthew 27:43; John 10:36); ". . . the only begotten Son dwelling in the bosom of the Father" (John 1:18); "I am the Christ of God" (Matthew 16:16); "I am the beloved Son in whom the Father is well pleased" (Matthew 3:17; 17:5); "Of a truth I am the Son of God" (Matthew 27:54); "All that the Father has is mine" (John 16:15); "He who has seen me has seen the Father" (John 14:9); "I and my Father are one" (John 10:30).[8]

The interested reader will also observe that Unity reduces the Lord Jesus Christ to the level of a mere man who had within him "the perfect Christ idea," and that "that same Christ idea is in every man." Thus it is taught by Unity that all men are miniature Christs, sharing in His nature and power. Should any doubt this assertion, we quote Unity's own literature to substantiate our contention: "Jesus was able to say 'All authority has been given to me in heaven and on earth'—we, too, can say truthfully that this authority has been given to us."[9]

Unity cannot deny that these are its teachings and that the Word of God in its entirety stands arrayed against such outright perversions of the true gospel.

---

[7] *Ibid.*, Vol. 57, No. 5, p. 464, and Vol. 72, No. 2, p. 8.

[8] Charles Fillmore, *Christian Healing*, p. 26.

[9] *Good Business*, July, 1949.

UNITY VERSUS THE ATONEMENT AND
RESURRECTION OF CHRIST

As Unity perverts numerous other Biblical doctrines, so does it attack the great and true teachings of the sacrifice of Jesus Christ. In the tradition of Mary Baker Eddy's Christian Science, Unity first of all denies the very obvious reason for Christ's atonement in the first place by maintaining that sin is merely "discordant belief" or "mortal mind," not rebellion against the laws of a holy God. To quote the Unity literature once again, which makes its stand very clear: "There is no sin, sickness, or death." [10]

Opposed to this outright denial of sin's existence we find the plain declarations of Scripture: "All have sinned, and come short of the glory of God" (Romans 3:23); "All unrighteousness is sin" (1 John 5:17); "If we say we have no sin, we deceive ourselves, and the truth is not in us" (1 John 1:8). How futile it is for Unity or any other cult to attempt to escape from the paralyzing reality that "sin is the transgression of the law," and "the wages of sin is death" (1 John 3:4; Romans 6:23)! The Bible clearly teaches that the atonement of Christ was the fulfillment of the Old Testament sacrifice of a lamb for the sins of the people (Exodus 12:5-14), and that Christ as the "Lamb of God" (John 1:29) made full and complete payment for all sin, forever, upon the Cross of Calvary, "once," and then seated Himself at the "right hand of the Majesty on high" (Hebrews 1:3). Through His holy and precious blood, therefore, we have peace with God (Colossians 1:20), "and the blood of Jesus Christ his Son cleanseth us from all sin" (1 John 1:7).

In sharp contrast to this Scriptural picture of the atonement, the Unity view projects itself in unmistakable language: "The atonement is the union of man with God the Father, in Christ. Stating it in terms of mind, we should say that the atonement is the at-one-ment or agreement of

---

[10] *Unity*, Vol. 47, No. 5, p. 403.

reconciliation of man's mind with Divine Mind through the super-consciousness of Christ mind."[11]

The original Hebrew and Greek languages of the Bible leave no room for the chopping apart of syllables, such as Unity practices on the English translations; therefore, linguistically speaking, the entire view they promulgate, based on a purely arbitrary dissection of the term atonement, is a monstrous farce hardly worthy of refutation.

Respecting the doctrine of the resurrection of our Lord, and of all men for that matter, it should be noted that Unity believes in and boldly teaches reincarnation in place of resurrection, as this quotation from their statement of faith amply demonstrates: "We believe that the dissolution of spirit, soul and body, caused by death, is annulled by rebirth of the same spirit and soul in another body here on earth. We believe the repeated incarnations of man to be a merciful provision of our loving Father to the end that all may have opportunity to attain immortality through regeneration as did Jesus. 'This corruptible must put on incorruption.' "[12]

One may see in this thoroughly pagan view that Unity, Theosophy, Hinduism, Buddhism, and countless other Oriental philosophies go hand-in-hand down the primrose path of reincarnation, which the Scriptures flatly contradict by declaring for the Christian, "To be absent from the body [is] to be present with the Lord" (2 Corinthians 5:8); and for the non-Christian, "He that believeth not the Son shall not see life, but the wrath of God abideth on him" (John 3:36). Innumerable passages of Scripture belie the concept of reincarnation, which brands Unity irrevocably as a dangerous non-Christian cult.

THE CHRISTIAN APPROACH

Many persons ask, "Conceding that the facts as you present them are true and that Unity is a threat to the

---

[11] *What Practical Christianity Stands For*, p. 5.
[12] *Unity Statement of Faith*, Article 22.

gospel of our Lord, how can we best meet Unity's challenge to our faith?"

To this question I propose the following plan of action to be adopted when one deals with Unity adherents.

1. Insist that, whenever Biblical terms are used, you define the words to mutual satisfaction. This is important because followers of this cult repeatedly misuse common Scriptural terms and thus mislead the unwary into believing that they agree with the basic gospel, which they do not, as their literature clearly shows.

2. Emphasize from the Scripture the personality of the living God; show how incorrect it is to believe in an "It" when the Bible teaches that God is our living, loving heavenly Father, and not just an impersonal principle. Remember, a principle cannot hear, think, see, speak, create, or save; but *God* does all these things and much more because He is a Person (Genesis 1:1; Exodus 3:14; 20:1).

3. Drive home the inescapable fact of human depravity (Romans 3:23), universal evil, and personal sin. Appeal to reason to show that God loves sinners but hates sin. "If we say we have no sin we deceive ourselves," says John (1 John 1:8). Ask the Unity adherent if he or she knows what can remove sin other than the sacrifice on the Cross. Stress the desire of God to receive acceptance from the sinner (Acts 17:30, 31) rather than to wreak fiery revenge upon him.

4. Finally, in a spirit of Christian love, tolerance, and patience, stress the need for redemption from sin, the awful penalty for rejection of the Cross, and the certain reward for obedience. Never attempt to win the argument forcefully, do not condemn unless on a Scriptural basis, and, last but not least, stand firm, "reprove, rebuke, exhort, with all longsuffering and doctrine," "contend for the faith, and preach the word." Always remember that "this is good and acceptable in the sight of God our Savior, who will have all men to be saved and to come unto the knowledge of the truth" (1 Timothy 2:3, 4).

In these closing days of grace, it is the duty of the Christian church to defend as never before the gospel of our Lord and the doctrines of our common salvation. That God, who is rich in mercy, may see fit to raise a powerful standard in this needy field, must be our earnest prayer.

Seven

SPIRITISM: FAITH IN THE DEAD

Spiritism (or Spiritualism, as it is often erroneously termed) is by far the oldest form of religious cult extant today, and it is certainly one of the deadliest to the human soul. The history of mankind quite graphically reveals that animism, necromancy, magic, etc., have been an integral part of human development since time immemorial and a part upon which the Scriptures speak precisely.

Today in the United States there are said to be in excess of 455 "churches" actively associated with the cult of spiritism, and a membership numbering nearly 200,000 adherents. In South America as of 1956 there were reputedly over three million practicing spiritists, holding numerous meetings throughout the continent despite opposition of the "state" religion of Roman Catholicism which controls most South American countries. (However, documentation is at present lacking to substantiate this claim.)[1] Since the First World War the religious horizons of the globe have seen the rapid rise of various forms of spiritism, a religion unique in that it offers contact *with* and information *from* "beings" beyond the grave. The crude seances exposed by Houdini, famous magician and great nemesis of fraudulent mediums; Sir Arthur Conan Doyle,

---

[1] Spiritism no longer makes statistical information available to the public, so we can only report the last available figures (1956).

creator of the immortal Sherlock Holmes; William James, noted philosopher, psychologist, and psychic research expert; and Sir Oliver Lodge, British spiritistic champion, have given way to extrasensory demonstrations that few informed analysts care to challenge.[2] In fact, so acute and complete is the recognition of supernatural sensitivity, communication, and spirit manifestations that one of our leading universities has set up a special division for the study of "extrasensory perception," or ESP as it is commonly referred to in discussion. One of the most spectacular shows connected with spiritism is known as "psychic surgery." This is the demonic art wherein a spiritist under the control of his "spirit guide" supposedly performs intricate surgical procedures without benefit of antiseptic, anesthesia, or surgical tools. I am acquainted with a woman who, before her rebirth in Christ, assisted in such operations. Although demonic in origin, the manifestations in such "operations" are startling: blood and smelly, slimy "curses" removed with a rusty knife or scissors from brains, eyes, backs, etc.

Let us examine briefly the background of this amazing cult, which holds a deadly fascination for the adventurous and uninstructed soul, to see if it merits recognition by Christians, and in what light we ought to evaluate this thriving body of zealots.

HISTORY

Of all the religious source books in the world, the Bible unquestionably gives the history of spiritism in a most concise and dependable form. As far back as the Book of Exodus, the Scriptures reveal that the ancient Egyptians were practitioners of occultism, magic, sorcery, and necromancy, which they employed to duplicate the miracles of Moses

---

[2] See *Evidences of Immortality* by Alda M. Wade, The Christopher Publishing House, Boston, 1956, pp. 55-79.

when that great servant of the Lord appeared before Pharaoh (Exodus 7:11, 22; 8:18; etc.).

The attitude of God toward those who practiced such forbidden sins is also clearly outlined in Scripture, for the Lord ordered the death penalty for all sorcerers (Hebrew, *Mekashshelah*), as recorded in Exodus 22:18 and Leviticus 20:27, to cite two concrete instances. The Old Testament also named among those cursed by Jehovah persons consorting with "familiar spirits" and "wizards" (see Leviticus 19:31 and 20:6) as well as "necromancers" (Deuteronomy 18:10, 11), etc.

In company with these violators of divine command, Daniel the prophet speaks often of the "magicians" (Hebrew, *Hartummim*), "sorcerers," "soothsayers" and "astrologers" (Daniel 1:20; 2:2, 10, 27; 4:4; 5:7; etc.) who specialized along with the Chaldeans in the art of interpreting dreams and visions. The prophet Isaiah (8:19; 19:3) also speaks of such ancient spiritists as casting "sorceries" upon Israel (Isaiah 47:9), and King Saul before his apostasy drove such practitioners from Israel (1 Samuel 28:3, 9), as did the righteous King Josiah after him (2 Kings 23:24, 25).

The Scriptures likewise bear record that King Manasseh's downfall came about as a result of his delving into spiritism (2 Kings 21:6; 2 Chronicles 33:6), and his ensuing practice of idolatry in defiance of the command of Jehovah. The Bible then presents a devastating resumé of man's forbidden desire to uncover the hidden spiritual mysteries of the universe, even if "witchcraft" (2 Kings 9:22; Micah 5:12; Nahum 3:4), "divination" (1 Samuel 15:23), or "enchantments" (2 Chronicles 33:6) must be employed to further his unholy quest. The Egyptians (Exodus 8:18), Babylonians, Chaldeans (Daniel 2:2), and Canaanites (Leviticus 19:31), Scripture tells us, all practiced spiritism. This practice in one form or another continued throughout the ages, until in 1848 it received its modern rebirth at Hydesville (Wayne County), New York, in the persons of Kate and Margaret Fox—two of the best-known of the eighteenth-century promulgators of spiritism.

THE ROCHESTER RAPPINGS

The Rochester Rappings,[3] as they have been designated historically, began in the year 1848, when strange rapping or knocking sounds were heard by two young girls, Kate and Margaret Fox, the former six years of age and the latter eight years of age. These unusual sounds emanated from the bedroom of the two children, and as a result of these allegedly supernatural manifestations of spirit influence, modern Spiritualism as a functioning cult gradually evolved. In later years the Fox sisters reputedly explained away the rappings as "childish pranks." However, as the evidence clearly reveals today, the damage had already been done, for out of these "manifestations" the Spiritualist Church in America developed; and scores of Spiritualist mediums arose to offer contact with departed loved ones as "bait" to attract uninformed souls toward the dark labyrinth of spiritism. It is interesting to note that spiritism has made its strongest appeal to those who have suffered great losses, and after each great war spiritism always appears to be on the upgrade following death of a beloved husband, brother, son, etc., as a result of national conflict. (See *Christianity Through the Centuries*, p. 460, by Earl E. Cairns, Zondervan Publishing House, 1954.) One of the great early prophets of modern-day Spiritualism was Andrew Jackson Davis, a poorly educated but extremely earnest disciple of "spirit communication." In 1847 Davis published his *Principles of Nature, Her Divine Revelations*, and *The Voice to Mankind*, which is reputed to have gone through over fifty editions in the United States. To this day Davis is revered by modern Spiritualists as one of the great prophets of the movement. In 1852 Spiritualism was introduced into England through one Mrs. Hagen, and in Germany in 1856 there were exhibitions of so-called

---

[3] A phenomenon which began in the Fox home at Hydesville, and continued when they moved to Rochester.

"spiritistic writings." Other famous "mediums" were Daniel Douglas Holm, William Stainton Moses, and Leonora Keiper. Chiefly through the work of these people, the famous British scientist Sir William Crooks accepted Spiritualism as genuine. Later Sir Arthur Conan Doyle, along with numerous other important personages, came to recognize Spiritualism as a genuine indication of the possibility of communication with the spirit world.

When this background is properly understood, one can appreciate the phenomenal growth and development of Spiritualism both at home and abroad. Today the National Spiritualist Association, with offices in Washington, D. C., sponsors missionaries, maintains a h e library, and organizes and arranges lectures and c mp meetings throughout the United States and Canada, a well as in other countries. The Spiritualists also have a sch l where they train their "ministers," the Morris Pratt Instit in Whitewater, Wisconsin, which offers a two-year course o. instruction to those qualified to undertake advanced training in spirit communication, etc. As of 1955, the National Spiritualist Association claimed 22 state associations, 437 active local societies, and 216 other societies meeting on an irregular basis. The Association also boasts more than 32 camp meeting associations, as well as 120 churches and temples evaluated in excess of two million dollars. There are purportedly 370 ordained ministers and 1500 public mediums active today, claiming a constituency of more than 1.8 million members[4] (see *The New Schaff-Herzog Religious Encyclopedia*, Vol. XI, pp. 51, 52, Baker Book House, Grand Rapids, Michigan, 1953).

The interested observer can see that Spiritualism or spiritism is a definite religious power to be reckoned with along with the many other rapidly growing non-Christian cults, and we would do well to pay close attention to the challenge it presents to the gospel of the Lord Jesus Christ.

---

[4] A decidedly questionable figure.

THE THEOLOGY OF SPIRITUALISM

As we approach the theology of Spiritualism we are conscious of the fact that we are dealing with a most nebulous subject; most Spiritualists are essentially at odds with each other on interpretations of theology, which makes a concrete analogy of their beliefs difficult, to say the least. We shall now briefly survey some general beliefs held by spiritists in common and compare them with the teachings of God's Word.

The Doctrine of God

"We believe in infinite intelligence" (*Declaration of Principles*, National Spiritualist Association, p. 20, *Spiritualist Manual*, Revision of 1940). This particular statement by the Spiritualists as to their belief regarding God is characteristic of all pantheistic cults, who rob God of His personality and reduce Him to an impersonal force which is diffused through all creation, and which in effect makes up all phenomena existing in the universe. One may find ample documentation for this fact by perusing the literature published by the Spiritualists. In fact, the second statement in their *Declaration of Principles* reads, "We believe that the phenomena of nature, both physical and spiritual, are the expression of infinite intelligence." That such a view is pantheistic, no one acquainted with Spiritualist literature will deny; and pantheism, regardless of how it is stated, is a denial of the personality of God, which the Bible affirms to be the very core of Christian doctrine. In the third chapter of Exodus, when the Lord spoke to Moses, He most distinctly identified Himself as a cognizant ego by stating, "I AM THAT I AM," and He added, "Thus shalt thou say unto the children of Israel, I AM hath sent me unto you." (See also Isaiah 44:6; 42:8; John 8:58; Revelation 1:8, 9.) From these statements it can be seen that God is a reflective Ego, a personal Being, and the God and Father of the Lord Jesus Christ, the Redeemer and Savior of all men, but "especially of those who believe." Spiritualists therefore categorically deny the doctrine of the Trinity as stated in historic Christianity, and believe instead in an impersonal god—certainly not the God of the Bible!

The Person, Nature, and Work of Jesus Christ

In their proper Biblical setting, these doctrines are emphatically contradicted by all Spiritualist publications, and no Spiritualist will ever admit that salvation comes solely through the vicarious sacrifice of Christ on Calvary. Further than this, Spiritualism teaches "We are punished by our sins and we will be happy if we obey the laws of life" (*Declaration of Principles*, Simplified Form, p. 21, *Spiritualist Manual*). Relative to the divine nature of the Lord Jesus Christ, Spiritualists affirm that He was "a prophet" and "an advanced Medium," but in no sense was He "God manifest in the flesh" (1 Timothy 3:16) for the redemption of man.[5] Throughout the length and breadth of Spiritualist literature one will search in vain for any statement glorifying the Lord Jesus Christ as Savior of the world; in fact, they ascribe to Him all things except the one thing that would rightfully entitle Him to all the rest—that He is the eternal Word of God, (John 1:1), the Savior of mankind and Judge of all creation, without whom there is no salvation (Acts 4:12). The Bible, in direct contrast to the position of Spiritualism, states that Christ was eternal (John 8:58), that He became flesh (John 1:14), and that He died to translate men from the power of the evil one into His eternal kingdom (Colossians 1:13). The Lord Jesus Christ also said, "I am the way, the truth, and the life: no man cometh unto the Father but by me" (John 14:6)—a statement denied most energetically by all Spiritualists of the past and present. The Scriptures warn us that "in the last

---

[5] See *The Two Worlds*, March 10, 1956, p. 8.

days perilous times will come . . . men will be lovers of their own selves," that they will "bring in destructive heresies, even denying the Lord that bought them." We are commanded as faithful witnesses for Christ not only to "preach the Word" with power but to shun their evil doctrines and "contend earnestly for the faith once delivered unto the saints" (Jude 3). Let us never forget that he who denies the deity, atonement, and resurrection of Jesus Christ, regardless of the homage he appears to pay the Lord, is, as St. Paul put it, an "enemy of the cross of Christ" (Philippians 3:18), and as such the wrath of God continues to abide upon him (John 3:36).

The Doctrine of the Atonement of Christ

This cardinal doctrine of the Christian faith has been attacked most strenuously by spiritists, none of whom believe that the Lord Jesus shed His blood for the remission of their sins; in fact, atonement by blood is most abhorrent to them. In Spiritualism one is redeemed from the power of sin by being punished in this life, or by passing through various stages of punishment in progression in the next life, until sins are atoned for. However, for the Christian "the blood of Jesus Christ, God's Son, cleanseth us from all sin" and "without the shedding of blood there is no remission"; or as the Book of Leviticus puts it, "It is the blood that maketh an atonement for the soul" (17:11).

Spiritualism has been most vehement in its opposition to the historic Christian doctrine of the atonement, but lest we be deceived by their pretended reverence for Christ, we should remember the historic denials rampant in their early literature and easily discernible today in their contemporary publications. When our Lord stood before Pilate, He indicated that He had come into the world to die ("To this end was I born"). Indeed, He laid much stress upon His death and His vicarious sacrifice for sinful men, and there are numerous references to this in His statements and in practically every New Testament book. Spiritualists deny this cardinal doctrine, and, for that matter, every other cardinal doctrine of the Christian faith,[6] not to mention the authority of the Bible, which is considered by them to be just another "holy book." Little more need be said about the issue in question. It is plain for all to see that their beliefs are decidedly unchristian.

The Physical Resurrection of Jesus Christ

Of all the doctrines Spiritualists deny, this is the one which seems to cause them the most difficulty and at times downright consternation. The Biblical position on the resurrection of Christ is quite clear. Paul states, "But now is Christ risen from the dead . . . " (1 Corinthians), and Luke 24:39 proves conclusively that Christ was not raised a spirit and did not have a spiritual resurrection, for our risen Lord said, "Behold my hands and my feet, that it is I myself; handle me and see, for a spirit hath not flesh and bones, as ye see me have." Directly contradicting this statement, Spiritualism holds that Christ was raised from the grave in a spirit form, or to quote them, "a spirit resurrection" (see *The National Spiritualist*, April, 1956, p. 4). They further state that He is now an advanced medium giving regular messages from the other world. The idea of a physical resurrection is repudiated by all Spiritualists, and therefore we must answer as did Paul: "If Christ be not raised, you faith is vain; ye are yet in your sins"—and so they are!

We could spend a great deal more time discussing the divergent views of spiritism, especially their view of reincarnation, which teaches that spirits who have passed on have become reincarnated in other bodies, a view which is also espoused by the cults of Theosophy and Unity, but time will not allow. We may conclude this theological survey of spiritism by drawing attention to the fact that as far as Spiritualism is concerned, the gospel of the Lord Jesus Christ in its historic context has been totally rejected. The

---

[6] *Op. cit.*, p. 8.

only thing Spiritualists have retained is a semblance of Christian terminology to which they have carefully assigned different meanings, a fact amply demonstrated by the *Spiritualist Hymnal,* which takes the classic gospel hymn "Just As I Am" and renders it this way (*ibid.,* p. 43):

> Just as I am, thou wilt receive,
> Though dogmas I may ne'er believe,
> Nor heights or holiness achieve;
> O God of Love, I come, I come.
>
> Just as I am, nor poor, nor blind,
> Nor bound by chains in soul or mind,
> For all of thee within I find;
> O God of Love, I come, I come.

They repeat this procedure with many other gospel hymns, especially those dealing with the Trinity, such as "Holy, Holy, Holy," where the triune name is completely omitted (*ibid.,* p. 49). Such action should serve to warn all who may be tempted to dabble in Spiritualism to beware, as it is directly opposed to the gospel of Jesus Christ and should be shunned as a deadly poison to the soul.

Probably the best resumé of what Spiritualism really stands for is given by the *New Schaff-Herzog Encyclopedia of Religious Knowledge,* Vol. XI, p. 52, which states, "They reject the doctrine of the Trinity and of the deity of Christ, and also that of the supreme authority of the Scriptures. They hold to the existence of an infinite intelligence expressed by the physical and spiritual phenomena of nature, a correct understanding of which and a following of which in life constitutes the true religion; the continued conscious existence of the spirit after death is a postulate, and with this goes belief in progress as the unusual law of nature."

A careful perusal of contemporary Spiritualist literature will confirm the truth of this condensed but succinctly stated resumé.

THE CHRISTIAN ATTITUDE

This is the attitude which the Bible as a whole takes toward the practice of establishing "contact" with the spirit world.

Today throughout the world, even as it was in the days of ancient occultism, men still dabble in a sphere so dangerous to the soul that God commanded death under the Mosaic Law for spiritistic mediums convicted of necromancy (Leviticus 20:27). Man's ancient and unholy desire to explore the realms of God's domain is very much alive, and today zealous Spiritualists are actively proselyting converts among any and all who will listen.

The true Christian attitude toward spiritism must be one of hostility, theologically speaking, tempered with the desire to win the cultist to a saving faith in the Lord Jesus Christ. The Bible irrevocably warns against tampering with the realms of existence beyond human comprehension, and, as in the case of Saul and Samuel's spirit (1 Samuel 28:14), the results usually evoke divine judgment of a severe nature. Therefore, let us beware of such forbidden dangers.

Another common danger which spiritism introduces is that of demon possession, since the Scriptures quite definitely reveal that demon power and influence is present in most genuine manifestations of spiritistic phenomena. No Christian should therefore ever allow himself to be exposed to demon influence if it can possibly be avoided, for their presence is direct testimony to Satan's part in the unholy seance; no intelligent Christian should be found in attendance in such forbidden Satanic rites. However, the Scriptures also teach that no believer can be indwelt by demons or possessed by demons, since we are the "temple of God," and "God's Spirit dwells in us" (1 Corinthians 3:16). But other dangers are still involved in such contacts, and they should be shunned at all costs.

It is imperative that Christians understand spiritism and its contemporary resurgence in the light of Biblical prophecy. Prophecy teaches us that "the doctrines of demons" will multiply in "the last times," and that this is sound evidence indeed that the coming of our Lord draws nigh. Let those who truly "love His appearing" be prepared for the rise of false cults and doctrines, that we may warn the "other sheep" and the Lord's flock of those "Having a form of godliness but denying the power thereof . . . " (2 Timothy 3:5).

May the Lord, who is ever ready to forgive and save, richly bless this phase of the ministry of His church, that through the unmasking of error the glorious light of the gospel may shine into the hearts of those whose eyes have been blinded by the power of "the god of this world" (2 Corinthians 4:4). When this occurs, the great gloom of demonic, spiritistic cultism will be dispelled, and spiritists will learn that "there is one God the Father and one Lord Jesus Christ," "who . . . ever lives to make intercession for us according to the will of God" (Hebrews 7:25). This will be the day of their deliverance from spiritism, the cult of the dead.

Eight

THE BAHA'I CULT

Unlike the other cults discussed in previous chapters of this book, the Baha'i cult is of foreign origin and can be traced to the country of Persia, where in May of 1844 a 25-year-old Persian merchant, Mirza Ali Muhammad, assumed the title of "Bab" (Gate) or a type of manifestation of some great divine personage outside the realm of time.[1]

The Bab derived much of his early support from the Shaykahis sect in Persia, and for six years taught his beliefs among many of the local populace. As is often the case, violence usually follows in the wake of "new" revelation, and in the case of the Bab the pattern held true, for in 1850 he was murdered by irate Mohammedans. He was but 31 years of age, and just beginning to ascend the scale of religious prominence in Persia.

According to the teachings which the Bab promulgated, he believed himself to be one of the great religious leaders of the world, and did not hesitate to compare himself with Moses, Zoroaster and Mohammed, a fact (as we have seen in the case of the Mohammedans) which cost the newly announced messiah his life!

Modern Baha'ism still considers the Bab a great religious leader, though he has definitely been supplanted in their affections by one Mirza Husayn Ali, better known to the initiated as Baha'u'llah ("the glory of God"), who succeeded to the messianic throne of Baha'ism upon the death of his unfortunate predecessor, the Bab.

---

[1] J. E. Esslemont, *Baha' Ullah and the New Era*, Bahai Publishing Committee, Wilmette, Illinois, 1951

In the year 1863 this same Baha'u'llah declared himself the one prophesied by the Bab some thirteen years earlier, the one who was "chosen of God" and "promised one of all the prophets" (see J. E. Esslemont, p. 38). However, this self-declaration failed to overly impress his own brother, Mirza Yahya, who denounced Baha'u'llah and allied himself with the enemies of the newfound religion, the Ski-ihs.

However, this nefarious plot failed miserably, and the Baha'i movement gradually evolved into what is today known as the Baha'i faith, a worldwide religious organization which continues to teach in the tradition of Baha'u'llah, who, despite his claims to immortality, was rather unceremoniously deprived of his earthly existence by the angel of death, who overtook him in 1892 at Bahji in Palestine. He was 75.

Today the Baha'i faith is active in over fifty countries and claims a membership of over one million followers, although Frank Mead's *Handbook of the Denominations* lists only 5232 Baha'is and 134 "centers" in the United States.

Upon the death of Baha'u'llah there were estimated to be over a half a million to a million members of the Baha'i faith in the world (J. E. Esslemont, chapter 1), but since no statistics have been released by the Baha'i religion in the United States in recent years, it is most difficult to ascertain the true figure of their membership.

Summing up the history of Baha'ism to date, Baha'u'llah was succeeded by his eldest son, Abdul Baha ("servant of Baha'i"), a most able apologist for the cult who added thousands of converts to the Baha'i faith and was its first really effective missionary to the United States.

Abdul Baha died at the age of 77 in 1921, and was succeeded by Shoghi Effendi ("guardian of the faith"), who was assisted by a dozen and a half other leading Baha'i figures in governing the activities of the cult in America.

It was Tertullian, the great early church father, who stated, "The blood of the martyrs is the seed of the church." And this has been proven true in the case of Baha'ism, for where this cult has been most severely persecuted, there it has met with greatest success. This one fact alone should serve as a warning to all misguided zealots who persecute others because of beliefs which are not in harmony with their own There is no excuse for violence, and as in the case of Baha'ism such action resulted in the rapid multiplication of a dangerous non-Christian cult, the Baha'i faith.

A GLIMPSE OF BAHA'I THEOLOGY

As has already been observed, Baha'ism has great affection for the religions of the east (Buddhism, Confucianism, Zoroastrianism, Hinduism, Mohammedanism), and since it claims to be the unifier of all religions, one might expect that it would be strictly antagonistic to historic Christianity—which it most certainly is!

To make this point very clear, one need only visit the Baha'i temple, a great nine-sided structure located in Wilmette, Illinois (near Chicago), where the Baha'is have enshrined the nine great religious leaders of the world (in their opinion), or more pointedly the nine great revelations of deity. These personages include Moses, Christ, Buddha, Zoroaster, Confucius, Mohammed, and of course Baha'u'llah, whom they consider to be *the* supreme revelation of God for all time.

According to the teachings of Baha'ism, "Christ was the prophet of the Christians, Moses of the Jews—why should not the followers of each prophet recognize and honor the other prophets?" (*The Wisdom of Abdul Baha*, p. 43). This type of thinking must of course lead to the only conclusion which is at all logical in keeping with their system of thinking: "The revelation of Jesus was for his own dispensation—that of the Son—now it is no longer the point of guidance to the world. Baha'is must be severed from all and everything that is past—things both good and bad—everything . . . now all is changed, all the teachings of the past are past. Abdul Baha is now supplying all the world" (*Star of the West*, December 31, 1913).

The observant reader can note from this example of Baha'i teaching that the Lord Jesus Christ is relegated to the position of just another teacher in the sacred collection of nine, and His great authority "is no longer the point of guidance to the world," according to Baha'ism.

In direct contradiction to this testimony the Scriptures conclude, "For in him dwells all the fullness of the Godhead bodily" (Colossians 2:9), and as Jesus Himself stated, "I am the Way, the Truth and the Life; no one comes to the Father but by me" (John 14:6). The message of Christianity is an exclusive message and cannot be lumped together with the other religions of the world for the simple reason that the claim of Christ was that of absolute obedience on the part of man to absolute authority on His part, i.e., He was God manifest in the flesh and as such allowed for recognition of none other but Himself.

It is to be noted that the Lord Jesus Christ did not say, "I am one of the ways, I am an aspect of the truth, I am part of the life." His was an exclusive claim: "I am *the* way, *the* truth, and *the* life." The whole New Testament is nothing more than an amplification of this gigantic claim, "Before Abraham was, I AM" (John 8:58). We ought never to forget in studying the New Testament Scriptures that the Lord Jesus Christ was most emphatic in asserting His authority as the God-man, for He repeatedly stated His relationship to man: "If ye believe not that I AM, you shall die in your sins" (John 8:24); "I am the door; by me if any man enter in he shall be saved" (John 10:7, 9). These are the statements of the most dogmatic man who ever lived and the greatest fraud who ever lived, *unless* the claims He made for Himself were true. In that case, obedience to Him becomes the primary concern of mankind for time and eternity. As Peter so aptly put it, "Neither is there salvation in any other, for there is none other name given under heaven among men whereby we must be saved" (Acts 4:12).

Baha'ism is content to embrace all the religions of the world in an attempt to amalgamate their moral and ethical teachings, while at the same time recognizing the credentials of their prophets. But this is not an acceptable condition for Christianity, for either Christ is Lord *of* all, or He is not Lord *at* all, and the Christian can never accept any religious leader's equality with Jesus Christ, who is solely and uniquely the Savior of the world, "God only begotten" (John 1:18), the eternal Word (John 1:1, 14) made flesh for the salvation of all mankind, "the true God and eternal life" (1 John 5:20 ff).

Reflecting upon the previously stated premise of Baha'ism, i.e., the unity of all religions, it becomes evident that Baha'ism must conflict violently with the basic fundamentals of the historic Christian faith.

For the average Baha'i, God is an impersonal force, a being devoid of personality who is nonetheless the sum total of all goodness, and whose existence predicates almost immediately the nonexistence or ineffectiveness of evil.

The Christian doctrine of sin is also categorically denied by the Baha'i faith, or, to quote Abdul Baha, "The only difference between members of the human family is that of degree. . . . Some are like the sick and must be treated with tenderness and care. None are bad or evil" (*The Wisdom of Abdul Baha*, p. 128). Since the Baha'i faith fails to recognize the essential spiritual condition of the human soul (Romans 3:23; compare Jeremiah 17:9), it follows that they offer no remedy for the cause of sin except education (*op. cit.*, p. 128) and gradual spiritual progression into different planes of purification after death, until at length the soul is lost in the identity of "God," i.e., the extinction of individual personality.

It is apparent that the doctrine of the fall of man (Romans 5:15-19), which necessitated the vicarious atoning death of the Lord Jesus Christ, the second Adam (1 Corinthians 15:45), is superfluous if not totally unnecessary in the thinking of Baha'is, who admit no transgression sufficient to condemn the soul and no supernatural savior who is able to deliver from the curse of sin and lead the repentant sinner to eternal life.

The cardinal doctrines of the Christian faith: 1) the absolute authority of the Bible; 2) the doctrine of the Trinity; 3) the deity of Jesus Christ; 4) the virgin birth; 5) the vicarious atoning death of our Lord; 6) the physical resurrection of Christ; 7) Christ's visible second coming to judge the world; etc., etc., are all categorically rejected by Baha'ism. (See *Kingdom of the Cults*, chapter 12). There is very little indeed that a true Christian can have in common with the faith of Baha'i.

RESUMÉ

Looking back over our survey of Baha'ism, we can learn many things about this strange cult of confused but loving people. First we can discern that, thought it is Oriental in its origin, Baha'ism has carefully cloaked itself with Western terminology and has imitated Christianity in forms and ceremonies wherever possible in order to become appealing to the Western mind. Secondly, Baha'ism is eager not to come in conflict with the basic principles of the gospel, and so Baha'is are perfectly willing that Christians should maintain their faith in a normal sense just as long as they acknowledge Baha'u'llah and the general principles of the Baha'i faith. Thirdly, Baha'ism deliberately undercuts the foundational doctrines of the Christian faith by either denying them outright or by carefully manipulating terminology so as to tone down the doctrinal purity which characterizes orthodox Christianity.

We cannot in a chapter of this length cover as thoroughly as we would want the many deviations from Christianity so apparent in the Baha'i faith; for those interested in a further study of this subject, a review of J. E. Esslemont's *Baha'u'llah and the New Era* gives a good introductory presentation from the standpoint of the Baha'is.

As is always the case, the refutation of Baha'ism must

come from a sound knowledge of doctrinal theology as it appears in the New Testament, for no Christian can refute the perversions of the Baha'i faith unless he is first aware of their existence and of their conflict with the doctrines of Scripture. We must therefore be prepared to understand the scope of the teachings of the Baha'i faith, their basic conflict with the gospel, and the means by which we may refute them as we witness faithfully for Christ.

The United States has become a great battleground so far as the cults are concerned, with more and more new varieties springing up each year, many drawing heavily upon Oriental sources to entrap naive and uninformed souls. It is the duty of every true Christian to become familiar with these spreading delusions (one of which is the cult of Baha'ism), and through this familiarity with false teachings to bear a powerful testimony for the truth of the gospel of Jesus Christ, in whom alone is eternal life and without whom there is no life or peace.

Baha's have much to commend them, particularly their social consciousness and general love for their fellowman, whom they are seeking to lead into a "higher revelation" and to walk with God as they think him to be. Baha'ism is a Persian import, a mixture of Hinduism, Buddhism, Zoroastrianism, and Islam which repudiates the absolute authority of Jesus Christ and teaches instead an autosoteric system of religion in which man literally lifts himself by his own bootstraps onto the right path to life. We close our survey of Baha'ism by stating the immortal words of warning from the pen of the wisest man who ever lived except for incarnate Deity, King Solomon, who wrote: "There is a way that seems right unto a man, but the ends thereof are the ways of death" (Proverbs 14:16; 16:25).

Nine

THE SLEEPING GIANT OF ORTHODOXY

The universal cry in our era, which appears to be stirring the sleeping giant of orthodoxy, is: "Where did the cults come from? What can be done to combat them effectively?"

As has been amply shown, the major cults outpropagandize and outgive evangelical Christianity in the support of their beliefs, and they threaten in no small way to endanger every mission field on the globe, which until recently was largely free from concentrated cult activities. Unfortunately, some Christians take the attitude of a gentleman I spoke with 25 years ago, who has still not changed his views, to my knowledge, and who enjoys the distinction of being one of the leading publishers of Christian books on the Eastern seaboard.

I approached this distinguished gentleman at the time, hoping he would accept and publish a manuscript I had written which was an exposé of Jehovah's Witnesses. The coauthor and I offered the manuscript for publication at no profit to ourselves, and we even offered to let the publisher remove our names from the book, as we were then unknown in the writing field.

Mr. X, as we shall call him, thoroughly read the manuscript, which we left with him. When we returned the next day, he had nothing but good things to say about it.

"The Christian public needs books like this," he said emphatically. "I have never seen a more thorough job of documentation than you have done on this subject—it should be a bestseller in its field. I personally wish every

Christian who meets a Jehovah's Witness could have a copy of this. I think you have done a fine job and I wish you success."

Upon hearing such lavish praise as this, we fully expected to see the book printed in a very short time, but we were doomed to quick disappointment, for we did not then know that a glib tongue often camouflages a quaking heart.

Feeling that at last we could speak of publication, we pressed Mr. X for details and received the following comment: "Please do not misunderstand me, gentlemen. Though I like the book I cannot publish it. You see, I believe that we ought to let the Lord rebuke the devil, and these cults are devilish, so I take the position of the Archangel Michael when he contended with the devil (Jude 9) and I just say, 'The Lord rebuke thee,' for I have no desire to be involved with Jehovah's Witnesses."

We explained to Mr. X that there was no legal risk in printing the book, as three lawyers had already passed favorably on its contents, and that he would make a reasonable profit on it because it was the only book ever written on the subject and was therefore a primary source for pastors and interested laymen. However, all our protestations were to no avail. Mr. X continued in his "let alone" theory despite Jude 3 and our pointing out to him that his use of Jude 9 was completely at variance with the contextual meaning.

Finally, in desperation, we attempted to find out if what we had suspected all along was true, and we pointedly asked Mr. X the following question:

"Are you afraid to print this book because you fear the reprisals of the Watch Tower?"

Mr. X colored noticeably, and raising his voice stammered, "I . . . I do not wish to become involved in litigation with any organization as big as the Watch Tower, so I say again regarding the cults, 'The Lord rebuke thee,' and that is my decision."

We left the presence of Mr. X with heaviness in our hearts, but as we passed out of his office we saw a sign over the door which added that touch of humor so often needed in dark situations. The sign read in large bold type: "If God is your partner make your plans big."

Here was a man who ignored the commands of Scripture without blinking, and yet expressed as his motto complete trust in the promises of God. This was indeed both humorous and paradoxical, but it gave us an unforgettable glimpse of a type of thinking all too prevalent in our day. Pious temerity, we believe, has no place on the battlefield of the heavenlies (Ephesians 6:12).

I feel there is a definite solution to the problem of cults, and I believe that this solution can be aided by an and all Christians willing to cooperate. Here are the facts which can greatly facilitate grasping the significance of cult problems.

1. The cults came from dissatisfied souls who, because they could not understand Biblical Christianity (or having understood it, rejected it) preferred instead the religious opinions of kindred souls.

2. The cults grew to their present proportions because persons of similar persuasions sided with the "underdog," and the Christian church as a whole failed to meet the challenged in a positive and unified way.

3. The challenge of cultism can be met only with a systematic program dedicated to a thorough education of all Christians, clergy and laity, in the basic tenets, approaches, and propaganda activities of the major non-Christian cults.

Clarifying this third step, I should like to outline a concrete solution to this growing problem which has been long ignored and only half-heartedly considered, and is thus today potentially the greatest threat of all to evangelical missionary efforts.

I founded and am the director of an interdenominational research organization, the Christian Research Institute, which is my concrete answer, a portion of the solution so desperately needed. The Institute's purpose is to supply primary data on all the cults and non-Christian missionary activities, both here and abroad. It is the function of this Institute to index the major cults and to supply resumés of their origin, history, and doctrines, with bibliographical material aimed at specifically refuting their respective teachings.

To Christian colleges and seminaries CRI has proven to be most valuable because it fills a great need. Though strong cult curricula are offered in *some* colleges and seminaries, not nearly enough are offered in general, since confusion on what cultists believe and a general inability to cope with them effectively in the pastorate is unfortunately much in evidence. To refute cultism, *the Christian public must know what cultists believe and why they believe it.* But more important, Christians must know *why they believe orthodox theology*, since it is mainly through the contrast of sound doctrine with heresy that error is exposed and refuted.

The Christian church today must face the fact that unless unified action is taken against the tremendous upsurge of cultism in both the United States and numerous foreign mission fields, the church in the next decade will be fighting for its apologetic life against an enemy whose growth is directly proportional to the church's failure to educate its members to the insidious doctrines of the cults. God grant that many will see this grave danger and rise up to the defense of the eternal Word.

CONCLUSION

In the fourth and fifth chapters of the Book of Judges, a most interesting and often amazing narrative is given of the children of Israel's trials and tribulations under the iron heel of Jabin, King of Canaan, and his merciless Captain Sisera.

At the very ebb of Israel's fortunes, God raised up Deborah and Barak, two faithful judges whose task it was to free the Jews from their terrible bondage. In the course of their campaign to raise an army from among Israel and her friends with which to oppose the common enemy, many obstacles were encountered by Deborah and Barak. These ought to bear close scrutiny by Christians today, since we face an even greater enemy in the non-Christian cults and their followers.

From among the Jewish tribes, Ephraim and Benjamin eagerly sought to lift the sword for their brethren in response to the command of Jehovah. They were followed in rapid succession by Machir (the half-tribe of Manasseh beyond Jordan), Zebulun, Naphtali and Issachar, mighty men of valor who loved the Law of the Lord and went up to do battle for Him. The Scriptures further tell us that even the river Kishon (Judges 5:21) aided the cause of these valiant men by sweeping those of Jabin's troops who fell into it to a watery grave. The outcome of the mighty battle that followed is known by all who read the Scriptures, for Deborah and Barak emerged triumphant over the hosts of Jabin, while *Sisera the ruthless was destroyed by Jael, who drove a sharp nail through his temple as he lay sleeping in a tent.* Israel was thereby freed from the bondage and tyranny of Canaan, as God once more delivered them from the hands of their enemies.

We might well close this scene here and be content with the knowledge that God worked all things together for the good of His people, but unfortunately the victory song of Deborah and Barak, while it abounds in shouts of joy and elation, also carries with it a lesson and a warning concerning those who betrayed their brethren by *not* obeying God's command, and by *not* going up to do battle for Him. Let us look briefly at some of these traitors, and the reasons they employed for not obeying God's command.

REUBEN

The tribe of Reuben declined to do battle for the Lord because it *was a divided people whose leaders fought among themselves for the prestige of serving the Lord in battle, but who secretly wanted, each one of them, the post of honor in leadership and at the same time the prerogative of shunning danger.* Reuben's tribe, therefore, was ineffective and divided, a group who looked upon their brethren with coolness and allowed the carnality of their earthly natures to overrule in their souls the import of God's command. *Reuben's tribe also offered the lame excuse that they could not leave their flocks to battle for God, but they forgot the very words of their own law, as it is written: "Man doth not live by bread only, but by every word that proceedeth out of the mouth of the Lord"* (Deuteronomy 8:3). Thus it was that Reuben *"sat still"* and did not go up to the help of the Lord.

DAN

The tribe of Dan pleaded inability to serve God on the land because they were a seafaring people and had only ships, not armies. However, this also was a poor excuse, for Zebulun was inclined toward the sea but waxed valiant in battle on the land, helping to overthrow Jabin, the

Canaanite tyrant. Despite the pleas of Deborah and Barak, Dan also did not go up to the help of the Lord.

ASHER

In full sympathy with Dan, the tribe of Asher also "prayed to be excused," saying that they must stay at home and repair the inroads which the sea had in some localities made upon their land. A very small excuse will serve a coward who would rather observe a battle than participate in it no matter how just the cause might be! The tribe of Asher elected to play that coward, and in the company of its fellow conspirators did not go up to battle for the Lord.

MEROZ

Finally, the Scriptures arrive at the city of Meroz, located very near to the site of the great conflict, a city where there was much sympathy for Israel and no doubt many Jews who could have obeyed God's command to help Him, but who saw fit not to go.

Those who dwelt in Meroz were no doubt prosperous, and could have aided the cause of the Lord, but they in turn followed Reuben, Dan, and Asher in refusing to listen to Deborah and Barak, and so by reason of their fear of Jabin's iron chariots they too turned a deaf ear to the divine command and slept peacefully throughout the din of battle.

To apply this Old Testament account to the modern-day attitudes of many Christians toward the mounting battle against false cults is one of the simplest of tasks, for it is perfectly analogous to the present situation which many apologists must confront in cult warfare.

The orthodox Christian church today has its share of Reubens who vie with one another for the privilege of resisting error, but who seemingly never get around to giving any systematic help of either vocal or monetary importance because they are too concerned with position and not concerned enough with the dangers threatening from the cultist wolf. These well-meaning people think in effect that cults are just another "bogey man" erected by overzealous Christians to tap their already pinched pocketbooks; hence the loud noises about support, but the conspicuous absence of it to all practical intents and purposes.

The Reubens of today concern themselves with what Council they belong to, or which Bible teacher they follow, but they seem totally unaware of the fact that in their zeal to guard the sheep they have overlooked the variety of wolves that exist, and cultism is indeed a thriving specie.

The Dans and Ashers of today also fit perfectly the mold of their predecessors, who would rather engage Satan on their own terms than invade his domain, as God commanded, and to meet him on God's terms. The modern Dans will not fight on "land" because they are seafaring; that is, they will not endanger themselves to fight in a medium of which they are unsure. The Danites of today are not prepared "to give to every man that asks of you a reason for the hope that is in us." They halt after preaching the Word; they are almost totally incapable of "contending for the faith." To such depths has the once-proud science of personal apologetics descended that now both layman and pastor find themselves hard put to refute the ever-swelling billows of insidious cultism.

In company with the Reubens, Dans, and Ashers, we come to the most inexcusable of all varieties of subversives, which is grouped under the title of the ancient Meroz (Judges 5:23).

It should be remembered that of the four groups mentioned in the fifth chapter of Judges, the inhabitants of Meroz alone were placed under a curse:

"Curse ye Meroz, said the angel of the Lord, curse ye bitterly the inhabitants thereof; because they came not to the help of the Lord, to the help of the Lord against the mighty."

The reason for this damning thunderbolt of divine judgment is a shameful one indeed, for of all those who could have helped the cause of the Jews, Meroz was the closest to the battle and probably the most singularly powerful, yet it did nothing "to help the Lord." There is a conceivable excuse, though weak at best, for the Reubens, Ashers, and Dans of the ancient type, for they could plead ignorance of the menace that threatened and the obviously existing distances which separated them from the camp of Israel; but for Meroz, which was close at hand and knew the danger, yet slumbered, God speaks only one verdict: a curse! There is nothing more terrible than the judgments of the Lord, and "it is a fearful thing to fall into the hands of the living God."

As the result of this curse, Meroz, thriving metropolis though it was, shriveled in a short time to a shadow of its former self, and at length even this shadow disappeared from the face of the earth. Such was the reward of those who knew the command of God and, though strong and able "to help the Lord," chose instead the ignominious fate of desolation under the righteous judgment of God.

Unfortunately, today there are not a few Christians who court the fate of Meroz, and invite the judgment of God in their own lives because, knowing the commandments of God to "earnestly contend for the faith" (Jude 3) and to "reprove, rebuke, exhort with all longsuffering and doctrine" (2 Timothy 4:2) the teachings of demons, they sit by in idleness and thereby *strengthen* the enemies' position. The Lord Jesus Christ once said, "He that is not with me is against me; and he that gathereth not with me scattereth abroad" (Matthew 12:30); and it was no less a teacher than the Apostle Paul who also energetically instructed us to "contend for the faith" and to "put on the whole armor of God, that ye may be able to stand against the wiles of the devil" (Ephesians 6:11).

There are many people today who feel that "preaching the Word" is a "positive" message, and that "contending for the faith" is a "negative" approach. But such is not the teaching of the Scriptures.

The Apostle Paul, who wrote a great part of the New Testament, devoted a vast amount of space to "sound doctrine," always comparing it with the false teachings of others, whom he termed "beasts" and against whom he frequently "wrestled." The Pauline epistles abound in attacks upon false philosophies (see Romans vs. Pharisees, Galatians vs. Judaizers, Ephesians vs. general error, Philippians and Colossians vs. Gnosticism, etc.).

The Apostle Peter never ceased to warn of those "who privily shall bring in damnable heresies, even denying the Lord that bought them" (2 Peter 2:1), and Jude describes them as "raging waves of the sea, frothing out their own shame; wandering stars, to whom is reserved the blackness of darkness for ever" (Jude 13).

Far from being a "negative approach," the task of apologetics is a vitally positive ministry, and one that was actively followed by the prophets, Christ, Paul, Peter, John, Jude, and many others. The Christian today who does not recognize this fact, or worse, refuses to engage in apologetics when he realizes its importance, is in direct disobedience to the revealed will of God and cannot forever escape judgment of a severe nature.

To those unfortunate followers of Reuben, Dan, and Asher we speak only the command of God, which is "that ye should earnestly contend for the faith which was once delivered unto the saints" (Jude 3). We speak to you as in the vision of old: "Come over and help us" (Acts 16:9); for all Christians are brothers in the great struggle against the erroneous doctrines of the major cults. There can be no wavering because one is unsure of the ground, and there can be no excuse that God will accept, for the command is plain: God wants courageous men to stand in the gap. "He that has ears to hear, let him hear" (Matthew 11:15).

Let us therefore cease the petty squabbles that split the camp of true Israel today; rather let us join our forces to resist the onslaught of corrupt doctrines so evident in cultism. And as we lift our hearts in faith and our lives by obedience to the divine command, we shall become aware that the "sleeping giant" no longer slumbers, but that he has at last grasped "the sword of the Spirit" and is even now coming "to the help of the Lord against the mighty" (Judges 5:23).

SELECTIVE BIBLIOGRAPHY FOR FURTHER REFERENCE

GENERAL WORKS ON THE CULTS

Gruss, Edmond C. *Cults and the Occult in the Age of Aquarius.* Nutley, N.J.: Presbyterian and Reformed Publishing Co., 1974.

Hoekema, Anthony A. *The Four Major Cults.* Grand Rapids: Eerdmans, 1963.

Martin, Walter R. *The Kingdom of the Cults.* Minneapolis: Bethany Fellowship, Inc., 1965.

Peterson, William J. *Those Curious New Cults.* New Canaan, Conn.: Keats Publishing, Inc., 1973.

Robertson, Irvine. *What the Cults Believe.* Chicago: Moody Press, 1966.

Van Baalen, J.K. *The Chaos of Cults.* Grand Rapids: Eerdmans, 1962.

REFERENCE WORKS ON SPECIFIC CULTS

Jehovah's Witnesses

Gruss, Edmond C. *Apostles of Denial.* Nutley, N.J.: Presbyterian and Reformed Publishing Co., 1970.

Gruss, Edmond C. *The Jehovah's Witnesses and Prophetic Speculation.* Nutley, N.J.: Presbyterian and Reformed Publishing Co., 1972.

Gruss, Edmond C. *We Left Jehovah's Witnesses—A Non-Prophet Organization.* Nutley, N.J.: Presbyterian and Reformed Publishing Co., 1974.

Martin, Walter R., and Klann, Norman H. *Jehovah of the Watchtower.* Moody Press, 1974.

Martin, Walter R. *Jehovah's Witnesses and the Trinity* (booklet). Minneapolis: Bethany Fellowship, 1954.

Schnell, William J. *How to Witness to Witnesses*. Grand Rapids: Baker Book House, 1961 (under former title, *Christians Awake!*, reprinted 1975).

Schnell, William J. *30 Years a Watchtower Slave*. Grand Rapids: Baker Book House, 1956.

Thomas, F.W. *Masters of Deception*. Vancouver, B.C., Canada, 1970.

Van Buskirk, Michael. *The Sandcastle of the Jehovah's Witnesses*. CARIS (Christian Apologetics: Research and Information Service), Anaheim, California, 1975.

Mormonism

General Works:

Jonas, Larry. *Mormon Claims Examined*. Salt Lake City; Modern Microfilm Co.

Martin, Walter R. *Mormonism* (booklet). Minneapolis: Bethany Fellowship, 1976.

Snowden, James H. *The Truth About Mormonism*. New York: George H. Doran, 1926.

Tanner, Gerald and Sandra. *Mormonisn—Shadow or Reality?* (enlarged edition). Salt Lake City: Modern Microfilm Co., 1972.

Tanner, Gerald and Sandra. *The Case Against Mormonism*, Vols. I, II, III. Salt Lake City: Modern Microfilm Co.

Tanner, Gerald and Sandra. *The Mormon Kingdom*. Salt Lake City: Modern Microfilm Co.

Works Dealing Particularly with the Book of Mormon:

Budvarson, Arthur. *The Book of Mormon Examined*. La Mesa, Calif.: Utah Christian Tract Society, 1959. Now published by Zondervan under title, *The Book of Mormon: True or False?*

3,913 Changes in the Book of Mormon. Salt Lake City: Modern Microfilm Co.

Works Dealing with Polygamy:

Young, Ann Eliza. *Wife Number 19*. Hartford: Dustin, Gilman, 1879.

Young, Kimball. *Isn't One Wife Enough?* New York: Holt, 1954.

Christian Science

Gray, James M. *The Antidote to Christian Science.* New York: Revell, 1907.

Haldeman, Isaac M. *Christian Science in the Light of Holy Scripture.* New York: Revell, 1909.

Martin, Walter R. *Christian Science* (booklet). Minneapolis: Bethany Fellowship, 1976.

Snowden, J.H. *The Truth About Christian Science.* Westminster Press, 1920.

Work Dealing Specifically with Biography of

Wilbur, Sibyl. *Life of Mary Baker Eddy.* New York: Concord Publishing Co., 1908.

The Unity School of Christianity

Martin, Walter R. *Unity* (booklet). Christian Research Institute (out of print)—See *Kingdom of the Cults.*

Quimby, Phineas P. *The Quimby Manuscripts,* edited by Horatio W. Dresses. New York: Julian Press, 1961.

Herbert W. Armstrong

Anderson, Stanley E. *Armstrongism's 300 Errors Exposed by 1300 Bible Verses.*

Benware, Paul N. *Ambassadors of Armstrong.* Nutley, N.J.: Presbyterian and Reformed Publishing Co., 1975.

Chambers, Roger R. *The Plain Truth About Armstrongism.* Grand Rapids: Baker Book House, 1972.

De Loach, Charles F. *The Armstrong Error.* Plainfield, N.J.: Logos International, 1971.

Martin, Walter R. *Armstrong.* Minneapolis: Bethany Fellowship, 1976.

INDEX